The photographs in this monograph were produced over an extended period of time, dating from 2004 to 2012. For most of this time, Morris was on assignment, covering politics for *TIME Magazine*. *Americans* also includes some of his personal work as well as the outcome of multiple road trips supported by the former editorial staff of the Italian magazine *AMICA*. Without everyone's generous support none of this work would exist.

With special thanks to:
Gaia Tripoli, Michele Stephenson, Alice Gabriner, Kira Pollack, MaryAnne Golon, Paul Moakley, Daniela Bianchini, Silvia Tedesco, Robert Stevens, Hillary Raskin, Enrico Dagnino, Charles Ommanney, Claudia Christen, Colleagues and staff at VII, Gerhard Steidl and all his staff at Steidlville (Göttingen, Germany).
And all my family.

First edition 2012

Edited by Gaia Tripoli and Christopher Morris
Book design by Claudia Christen

Production: Gerhard Steidl, Bernard Fischer
Printing by Steidl, Göttingen, Germany

Steidl
Düstere Strasse 4
37073 Göttingen
Germany
Phone + 49 551 49 60 60
Fax + 49 551 49 60 649
Email mail@steidl.de
www.steidl.de
www.steidlville.com

ISBN 978-3-86930-448-9

Printed in Germany by Steidl

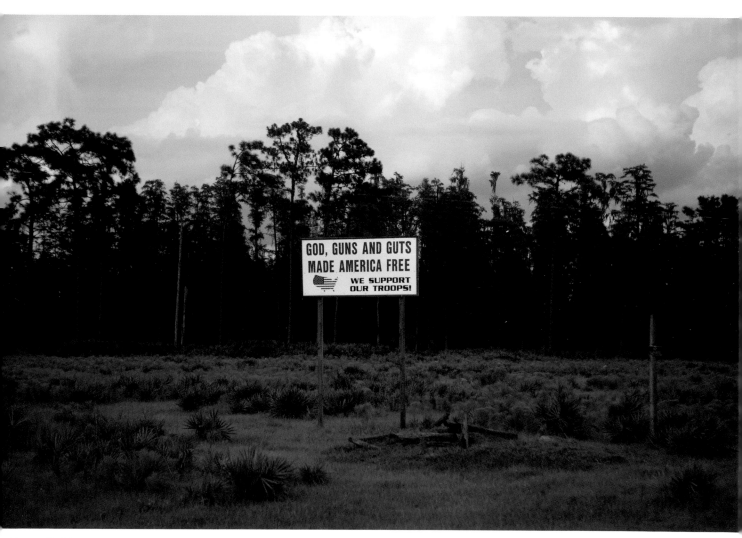

Tampa, Florida 2007

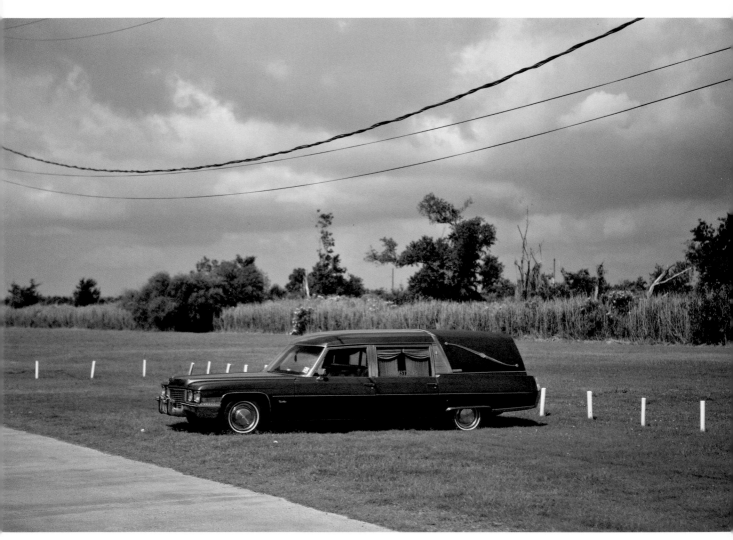

Venice, Louisiana 2010

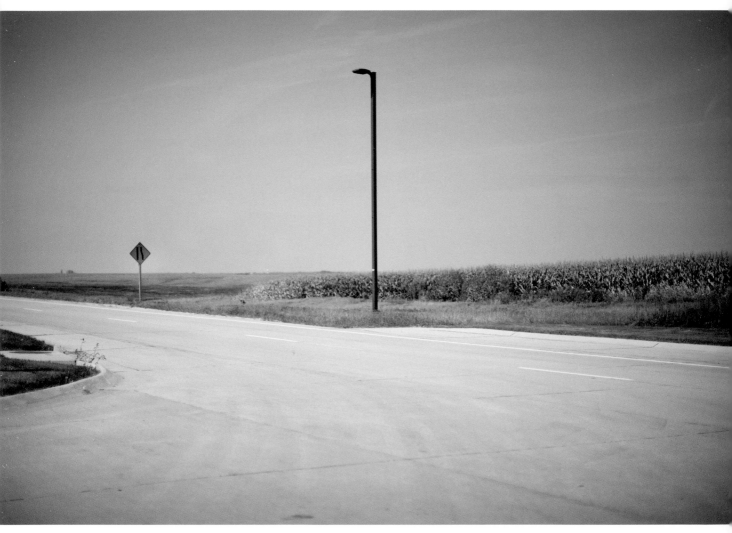

Cedar Rapids, Iowa 2008

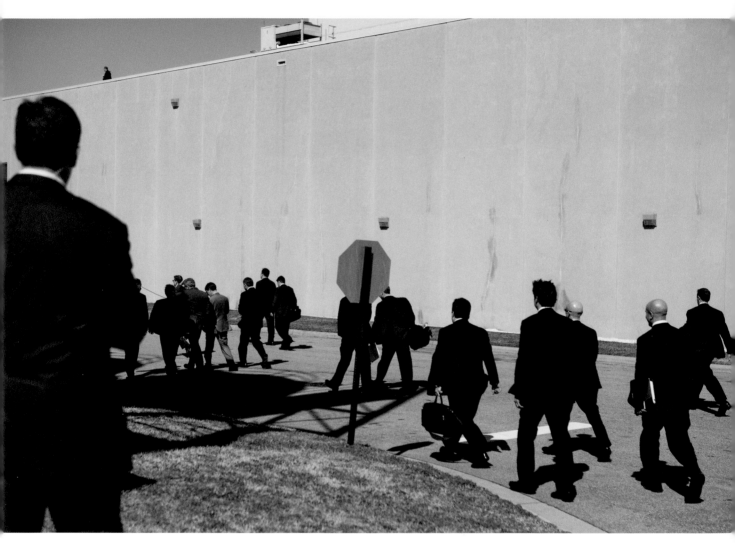

Franklinton, North Carolina 2007

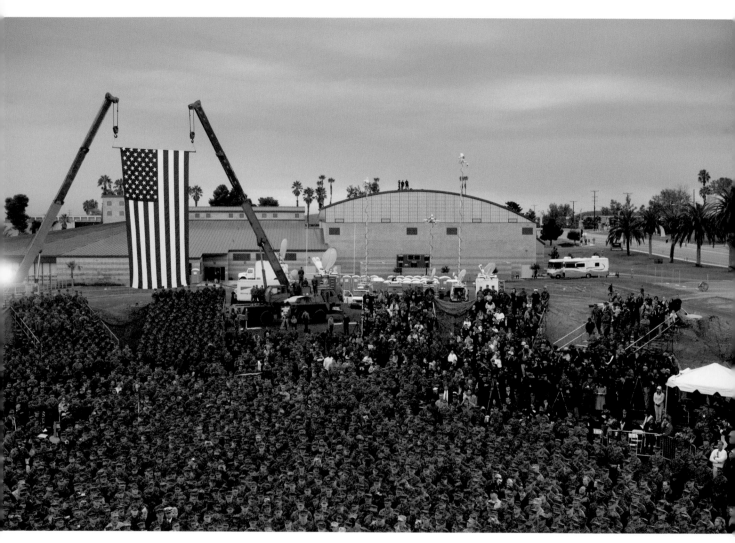

Camp Pendelton, California 2004

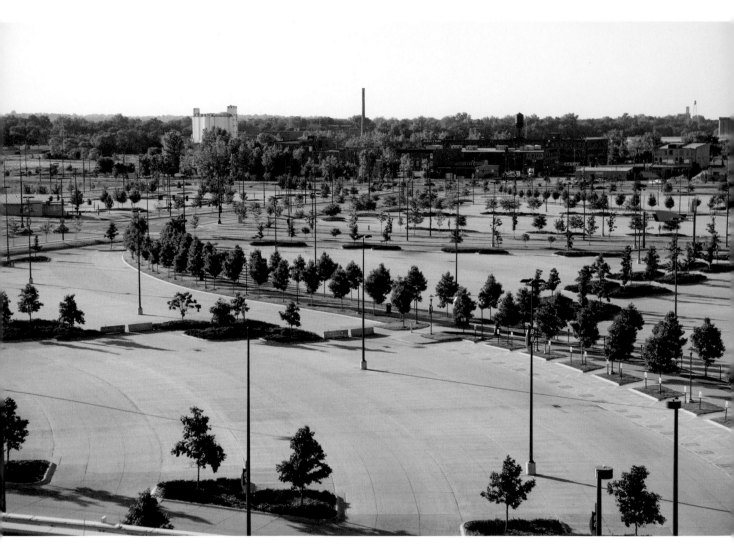

Omaha, Nebraska 2006

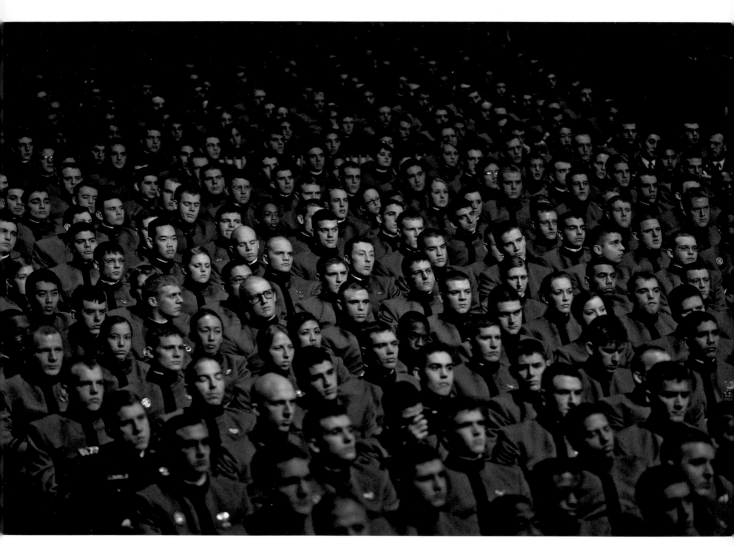

West Point, New York 2009

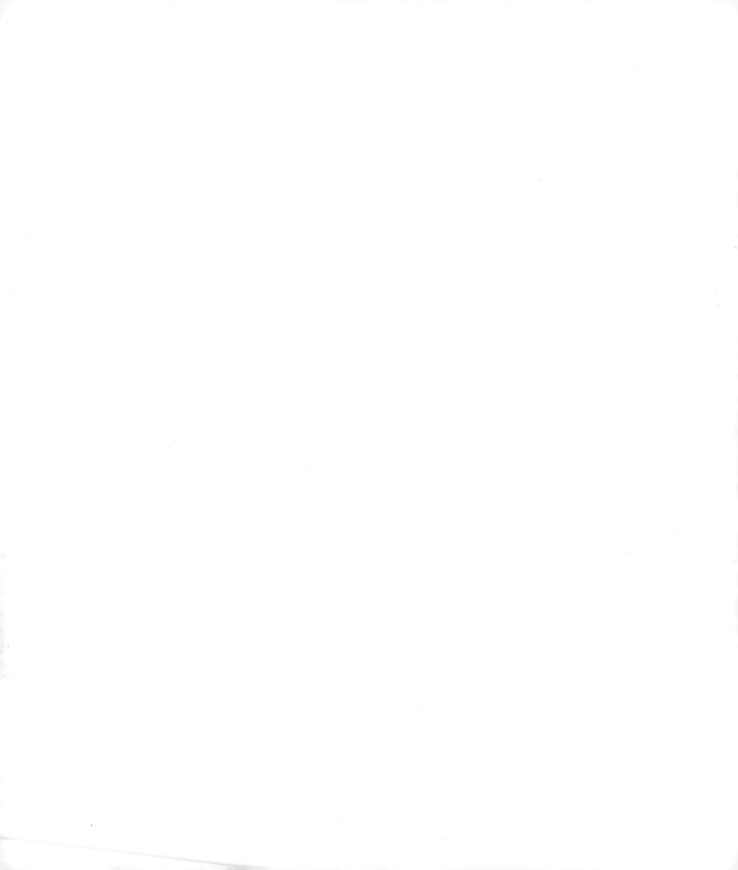

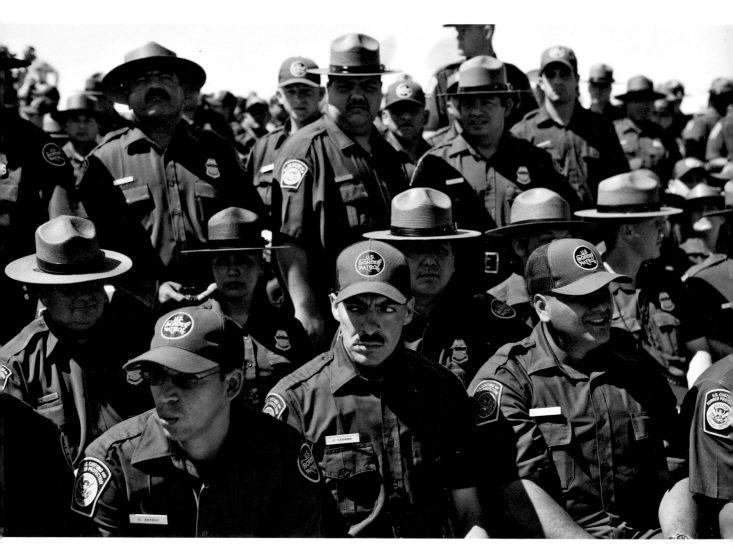

Atresia, New Mexico 2006

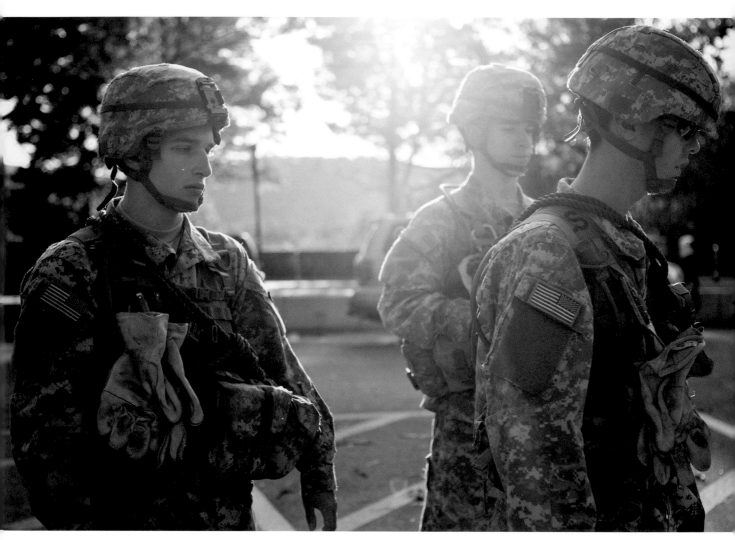

West Point, New York 2010

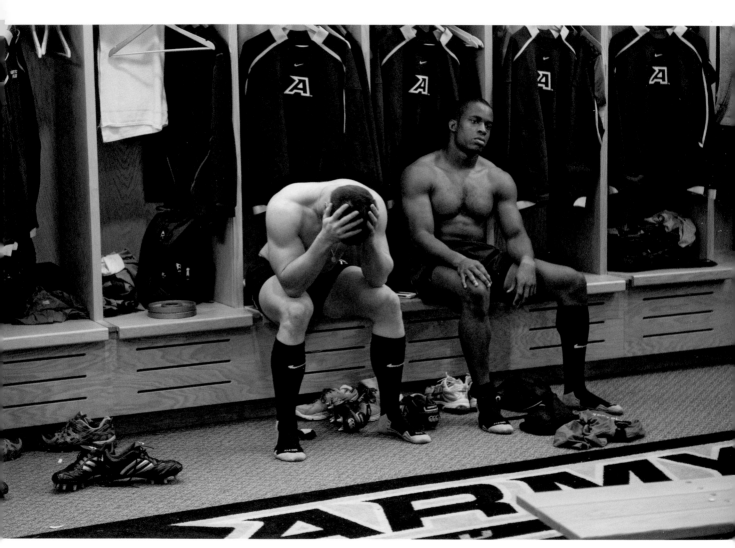

West Point, New York 2010

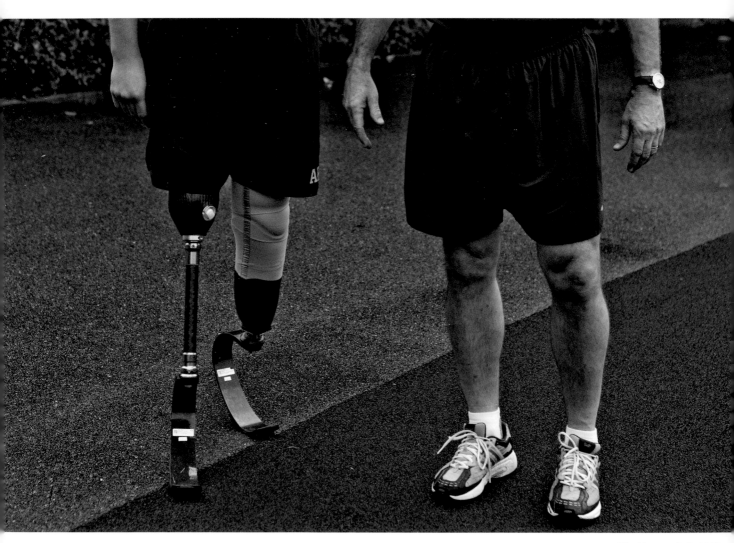

Washington, D.C. 2006

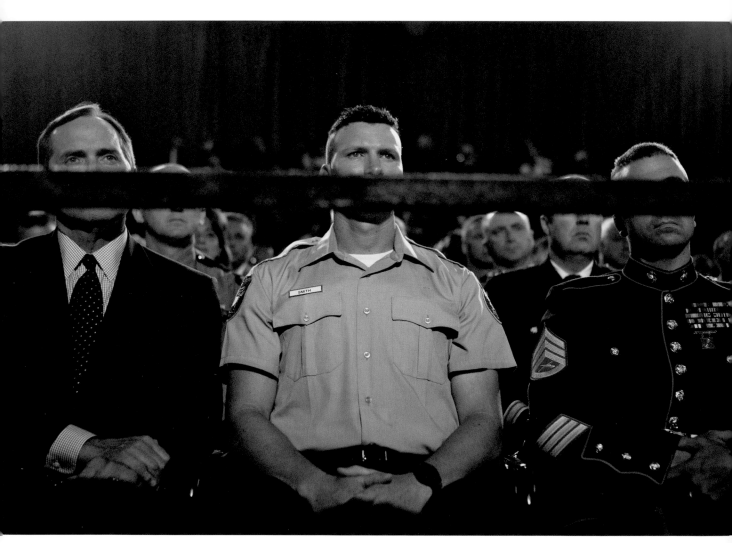

Columbus, Ohio 2005

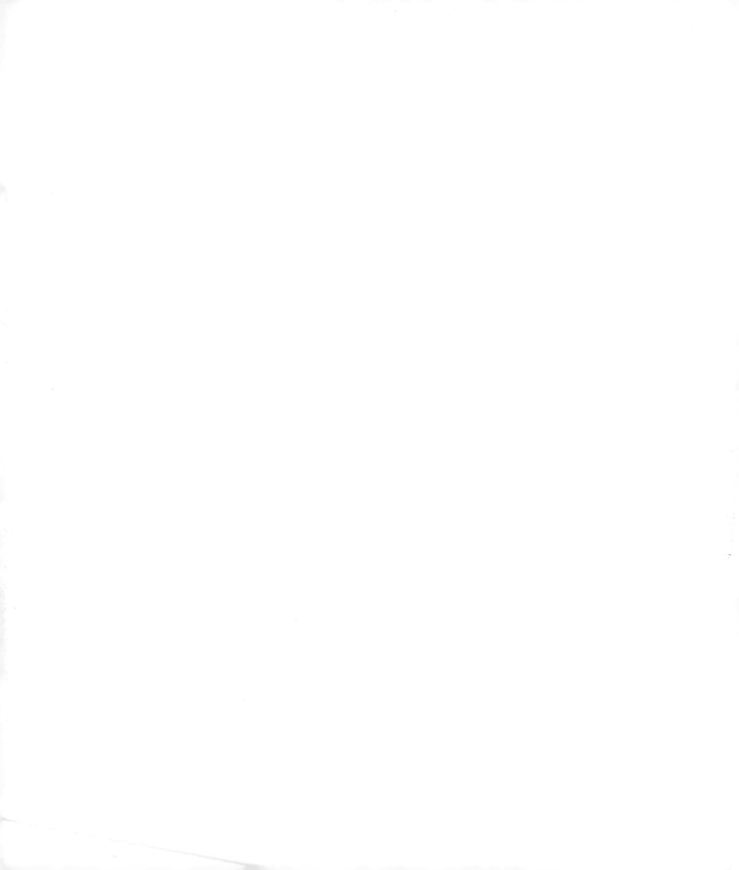

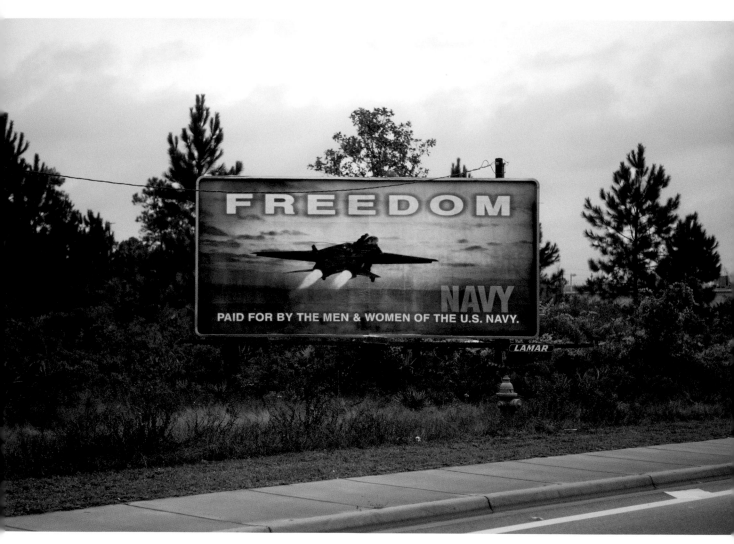

FREEDOM

NAVY

PAID FOR BY THE MEN & WOMEN OF THE U.S. NAVY.

LAMAR

Panama City, Florida 2008

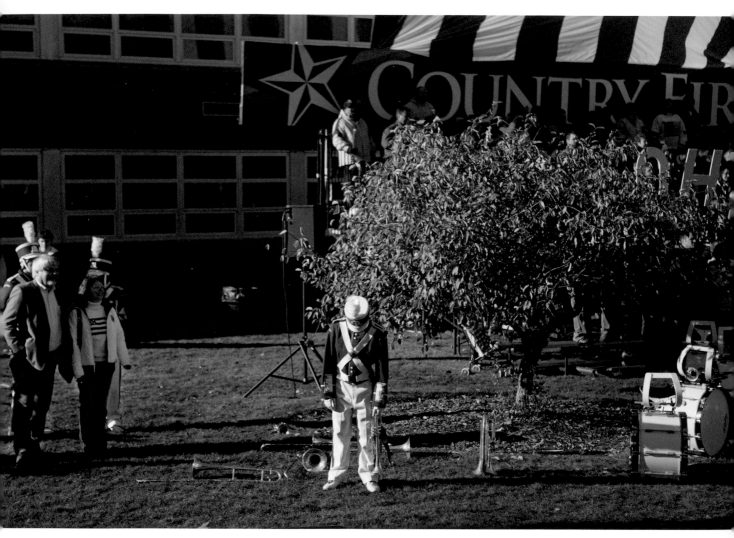

Defiance, Ohio 2008

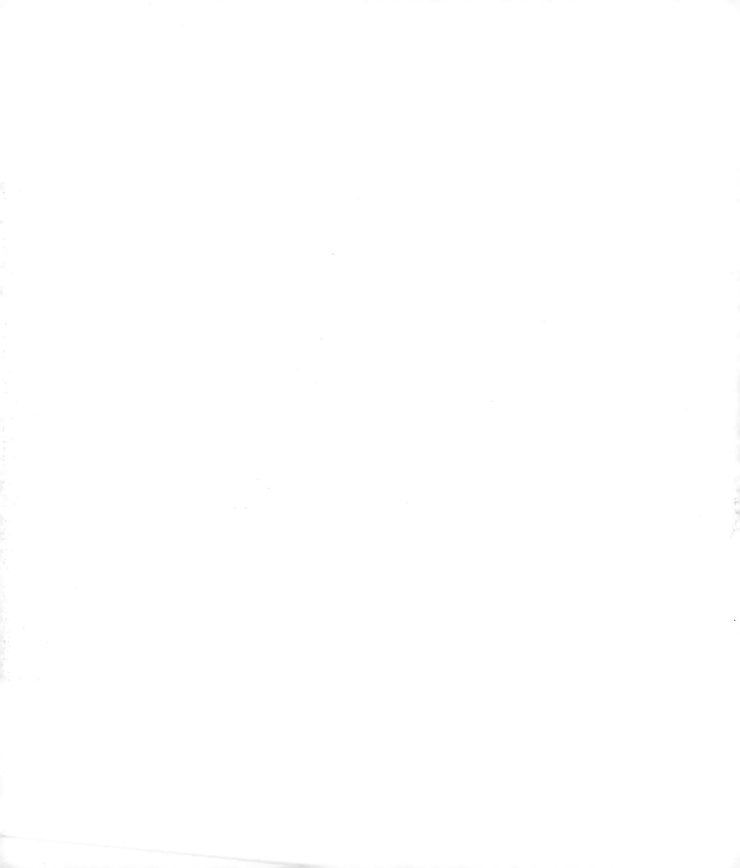

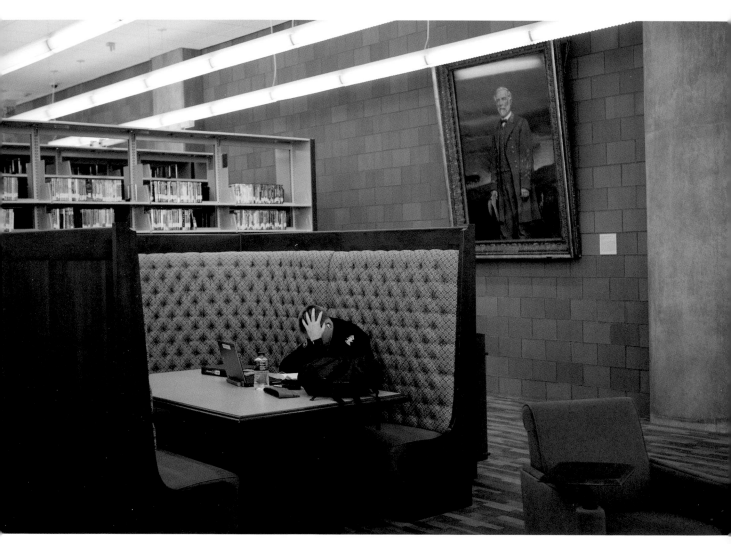

West Point, New York 2010

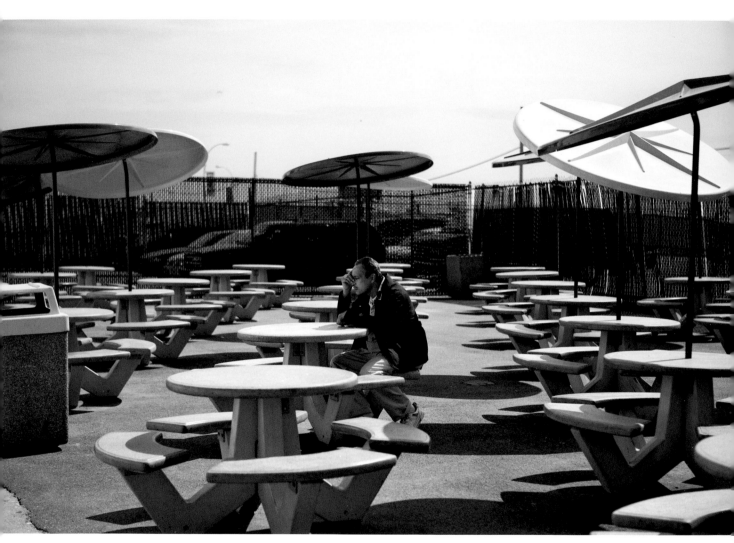

Coney Island, New York 2009

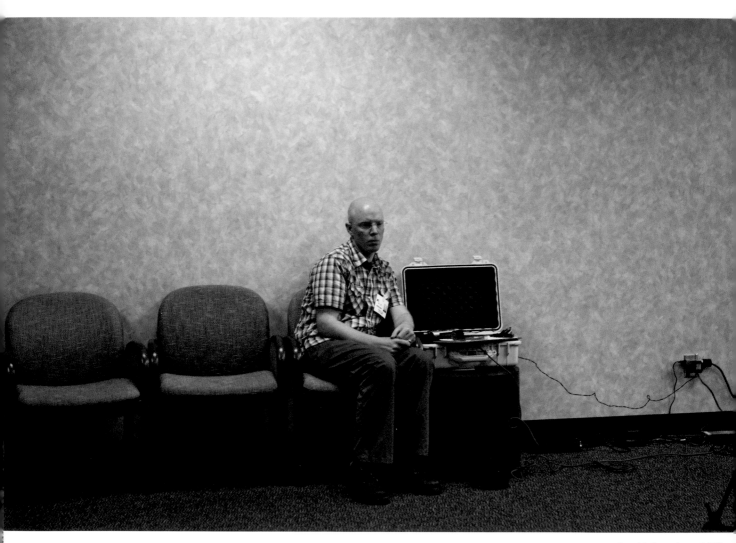

Des Moines, Iowa 2007

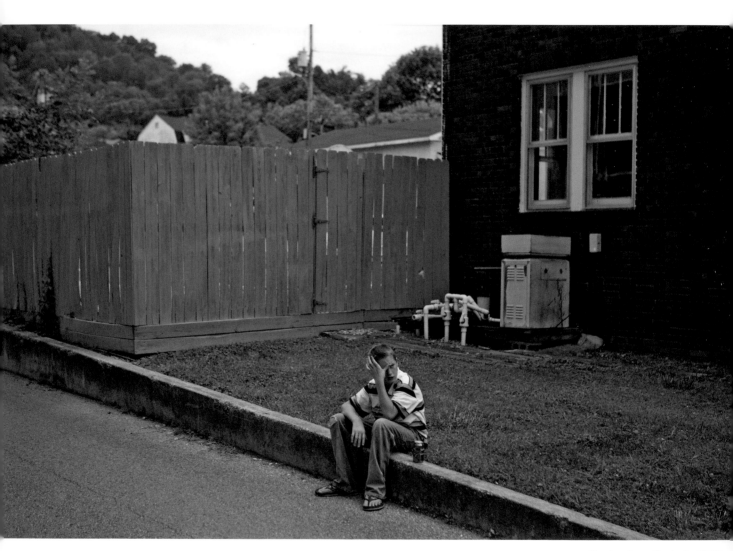

Prestonsburg, Kentucky 2007

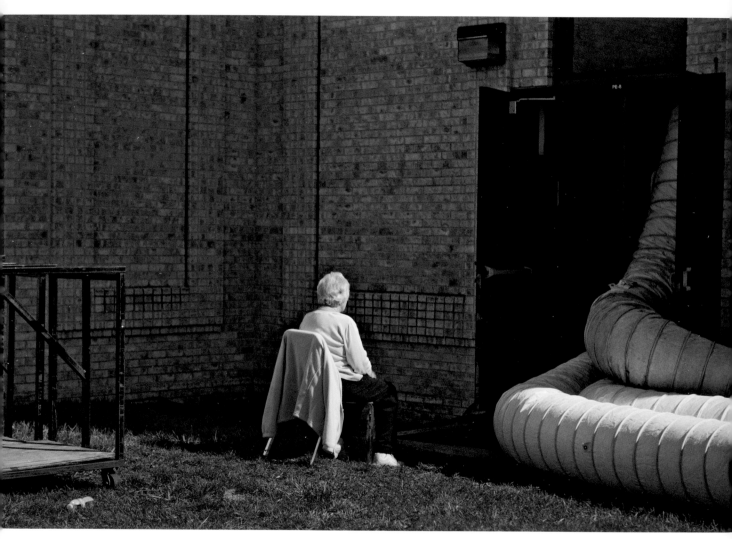

Blue Bell, Pennsylvania 2008

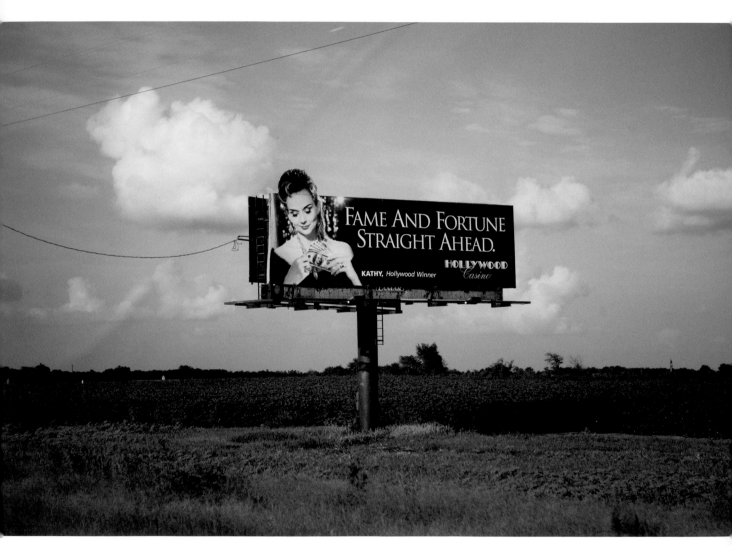

Highway 55, Mississippi 2007

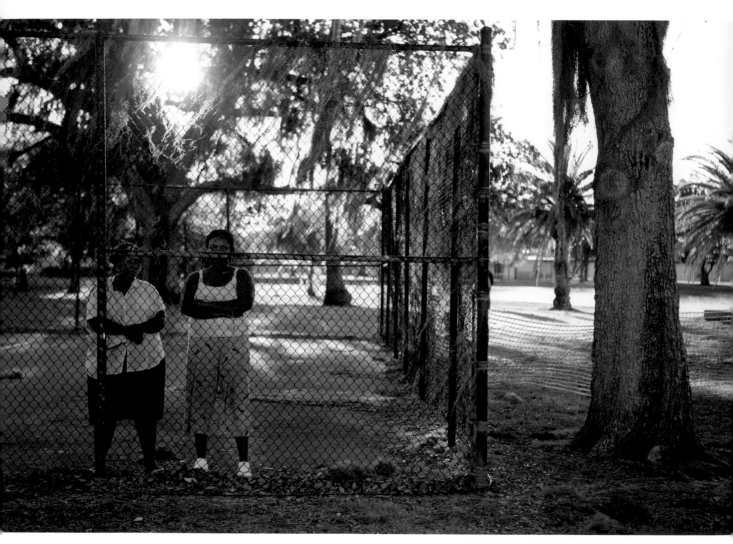

Sanford, Florida 2012

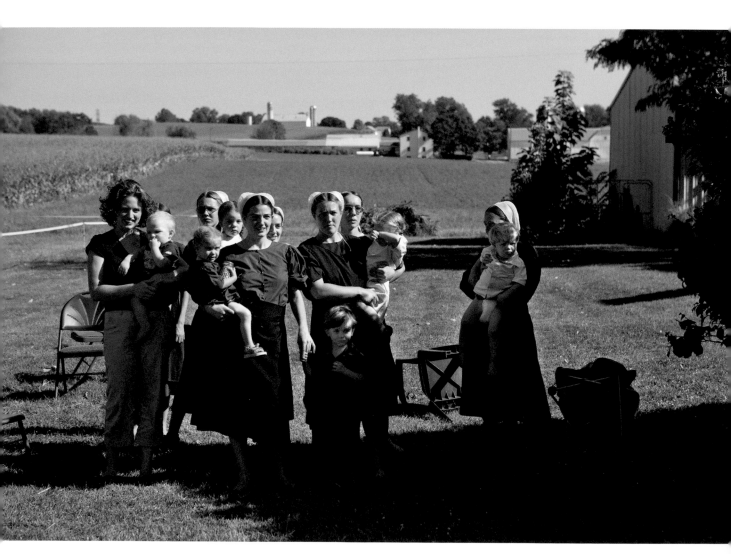

Lancaster, Pennsylvania 2006

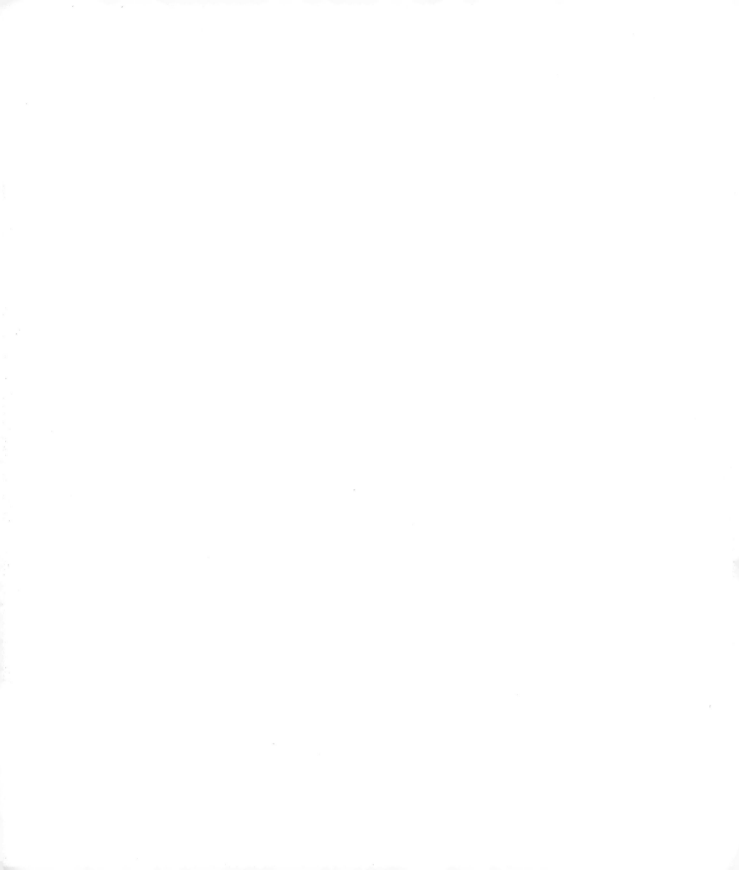

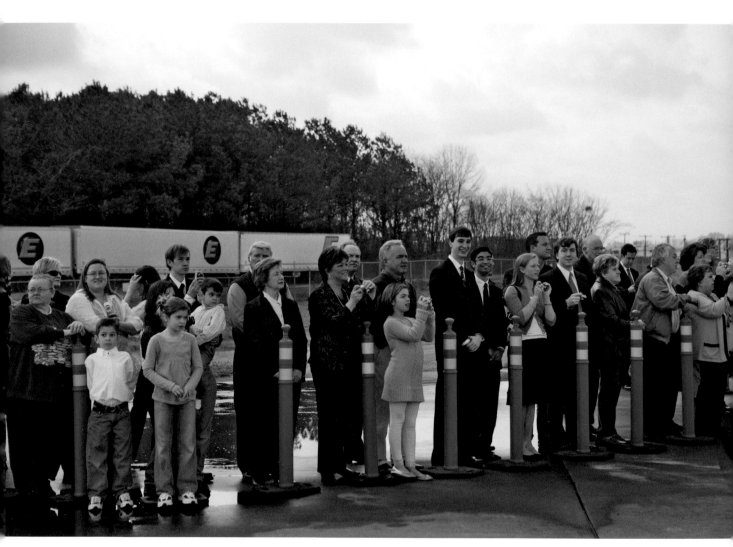

Chattanooga, Tennessee 2007

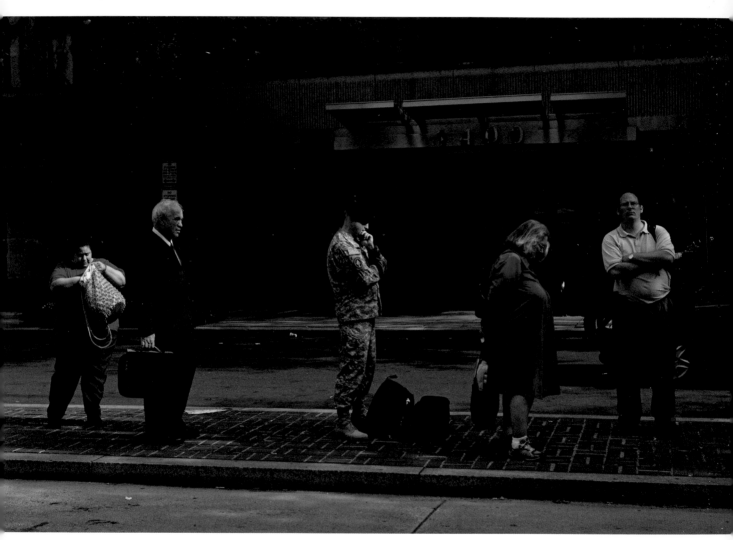

Washington, D.C. 2006

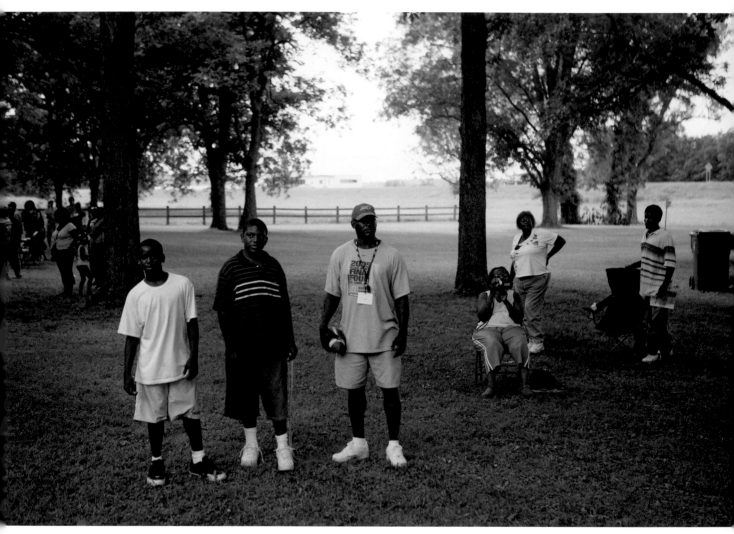

Marks, Mississippi 2007

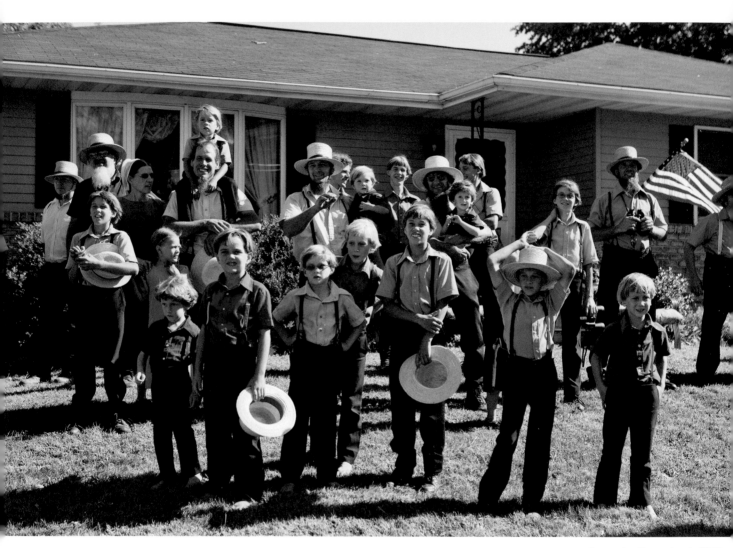

Lancaster, Pennsylvania 2006

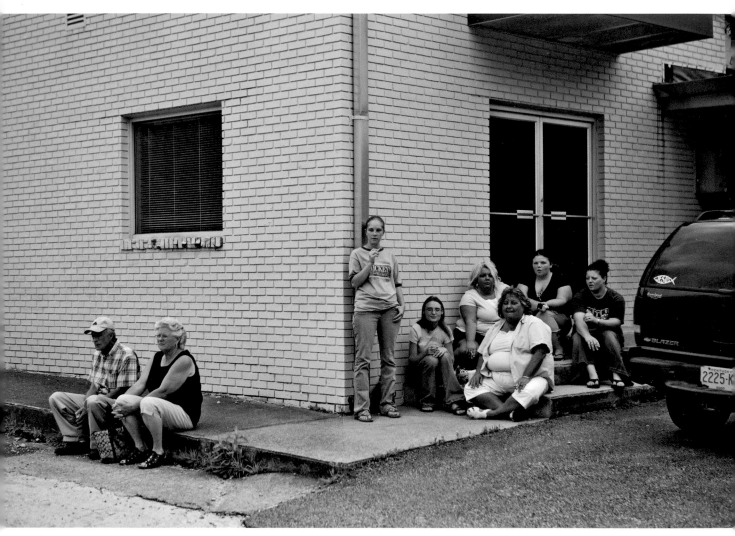

Whitesburg, Kentuky 2007

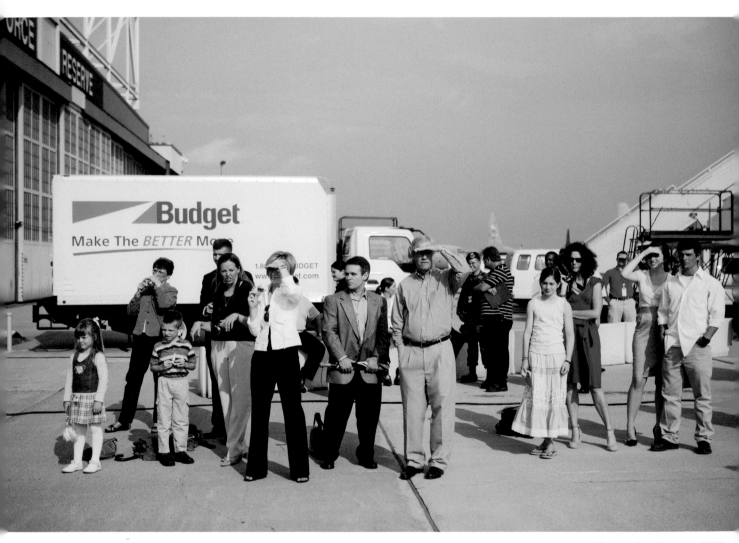

Minneapolis, Minnesota 2007

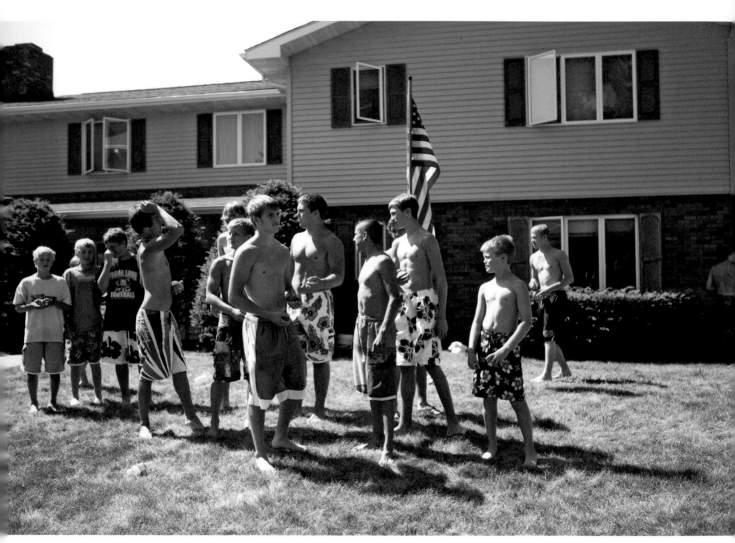

Clear Lake, Iowa 2007

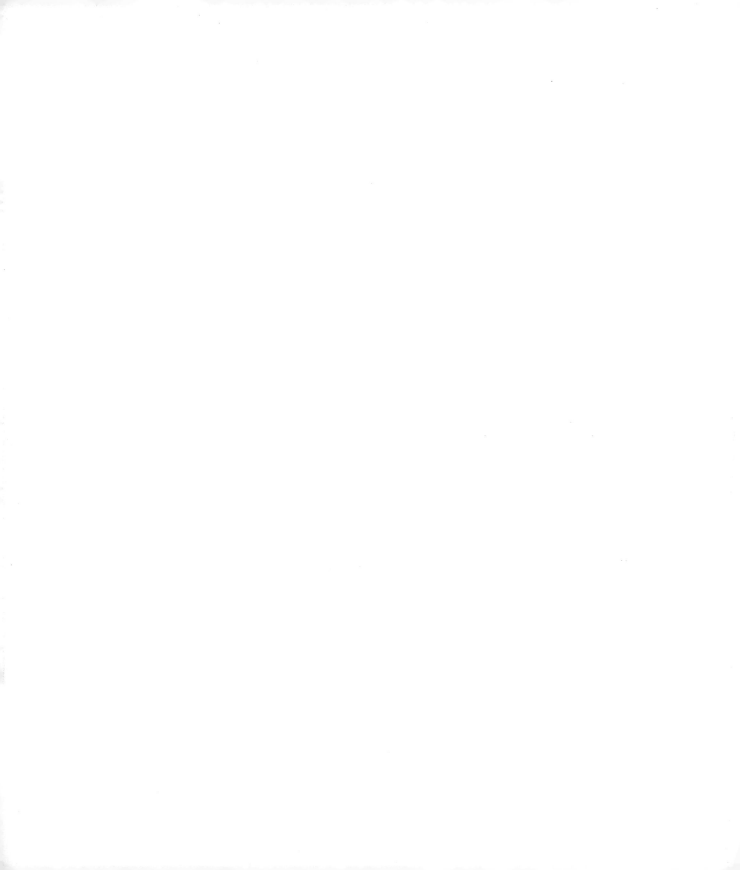

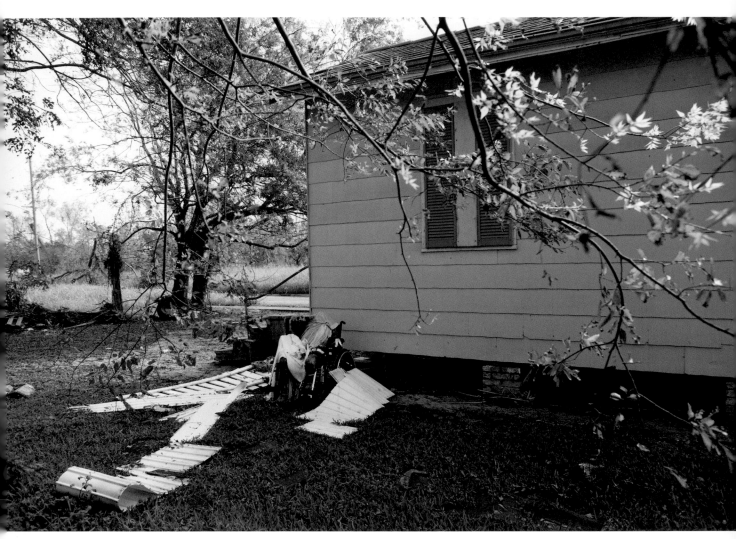

St. Bernard Parish, Louisiana 2005

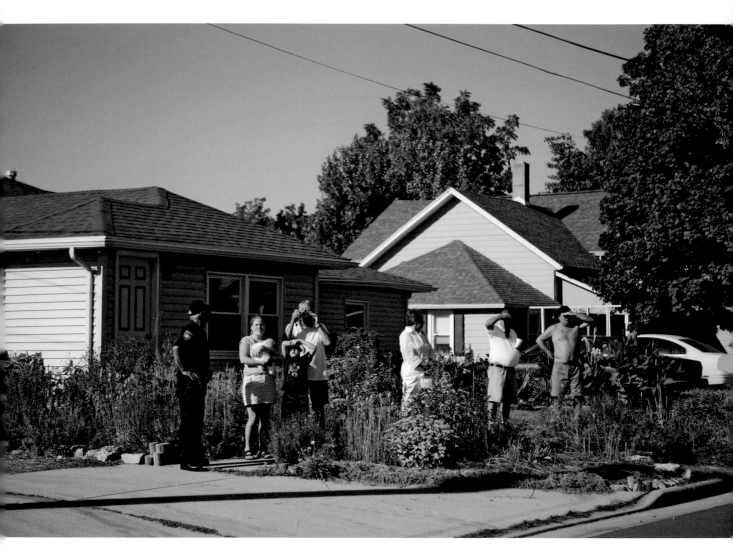

Obetz, Ohio 2008

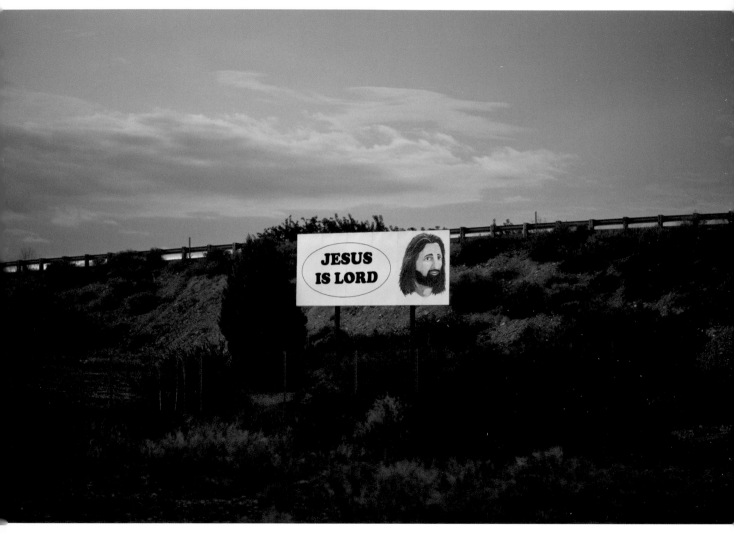

Camp Verde, Arizona 2008

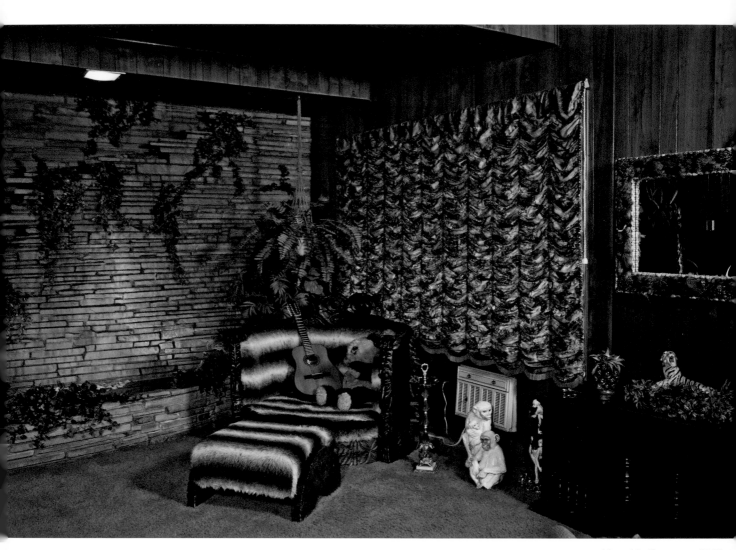

Memphis, Tennessee 2006

White House, Washington, D.C. 2008

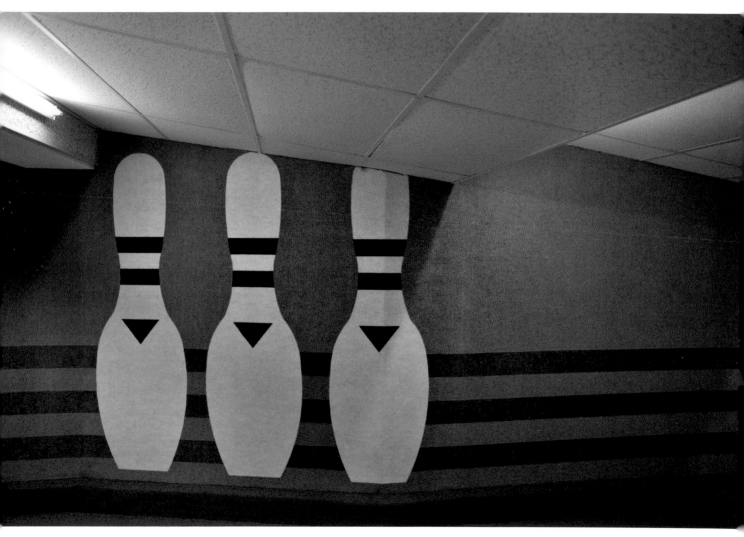

White House, Washington, D.C. 2008

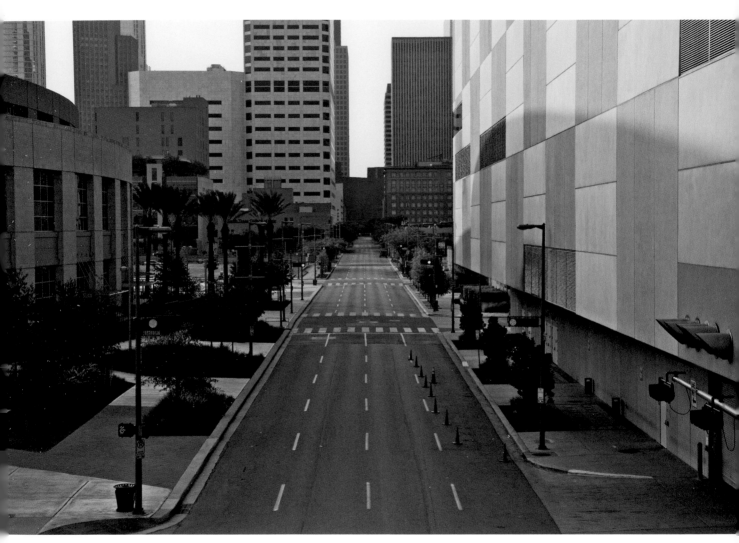

Houston, Texas 2005

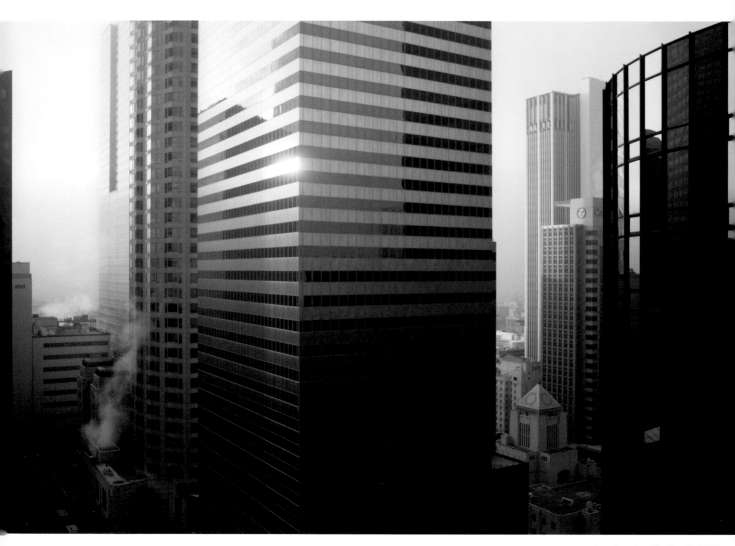

Los Angeles, California 2008

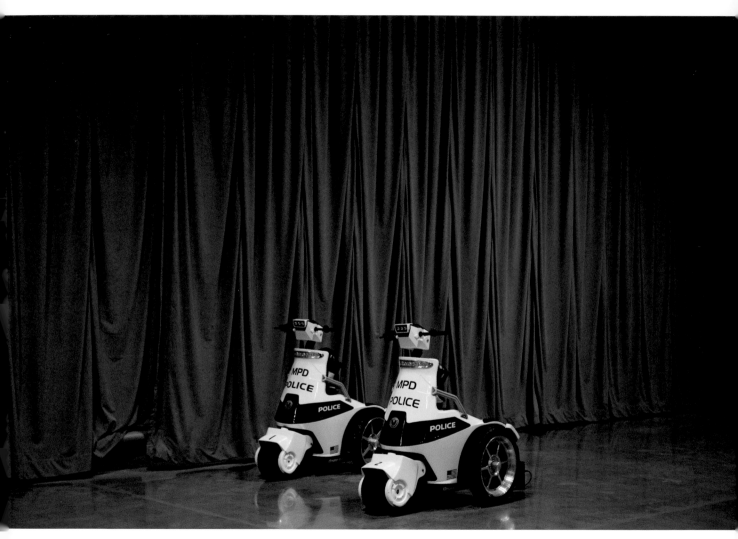

Minneapolis, Minnesota 2008

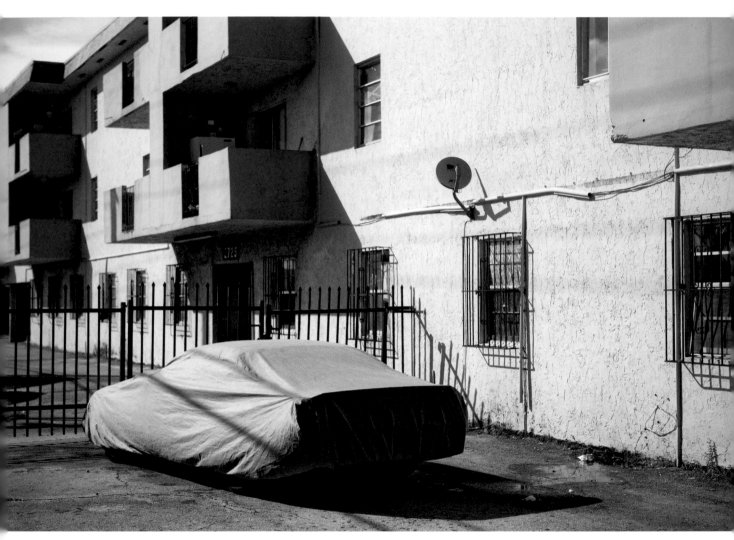

Fort Lauderdale, Florida 2010

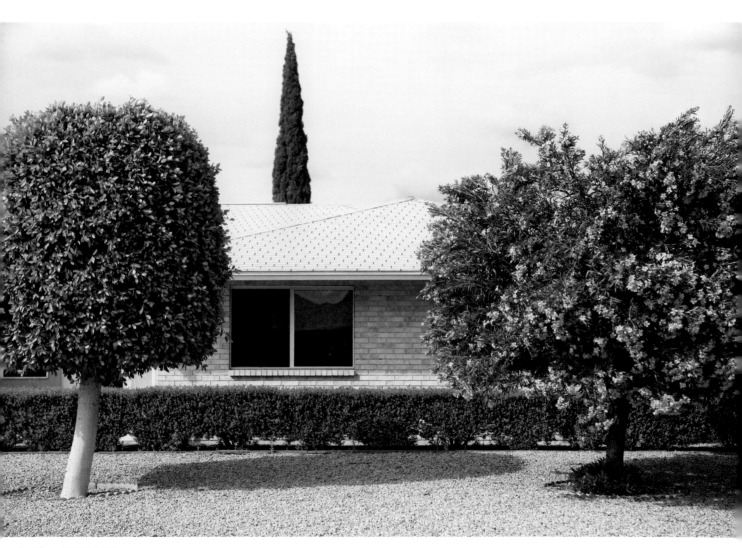

Sun City, Arizona 2010

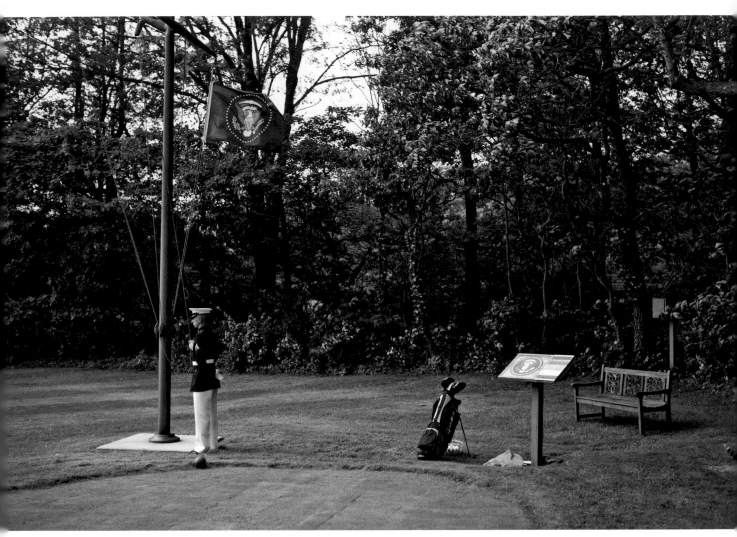

Camp David, Maryland 2008

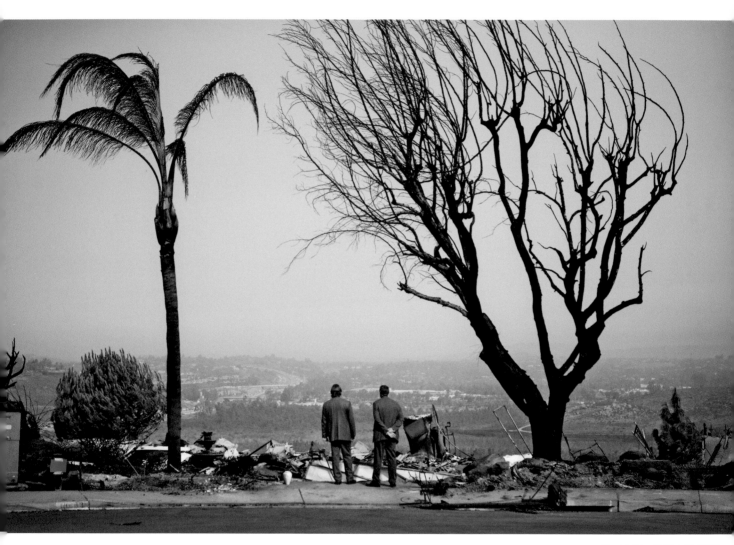

Escondido, California 2007

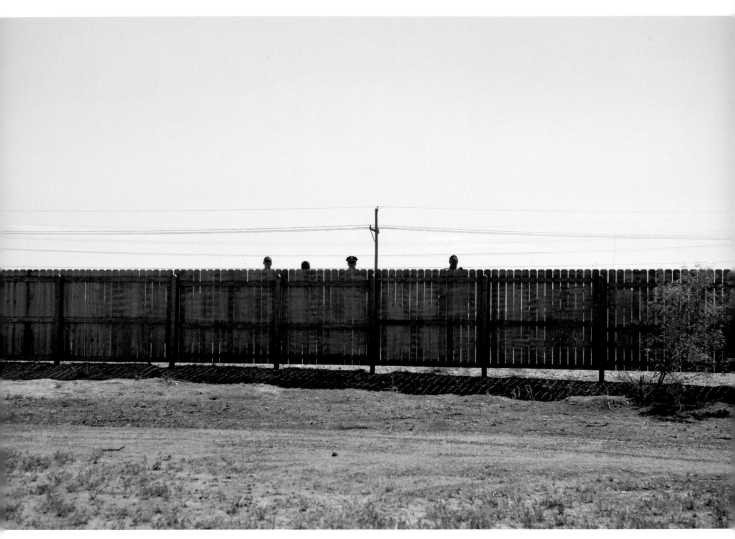

Artesia, New Mexico 2006

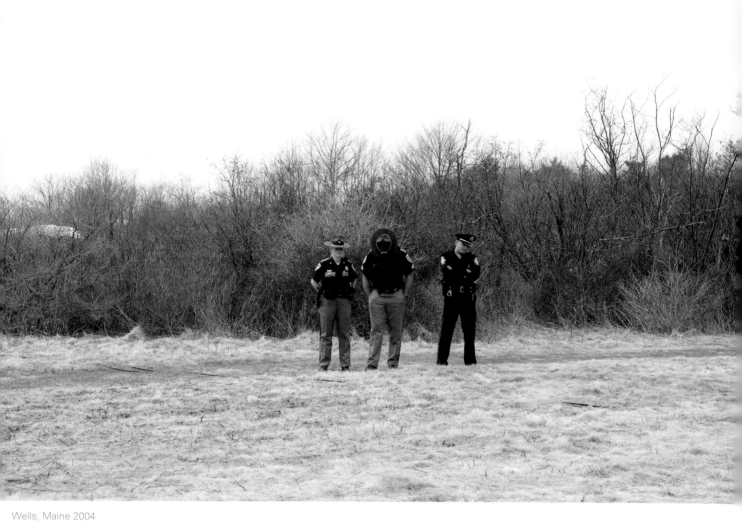

Wells, Maine 2004

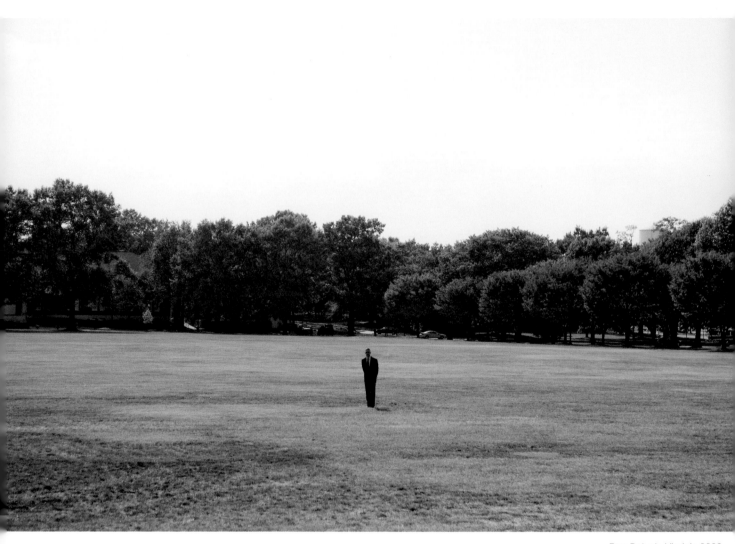

Fort Belvoir, Virginia 2006

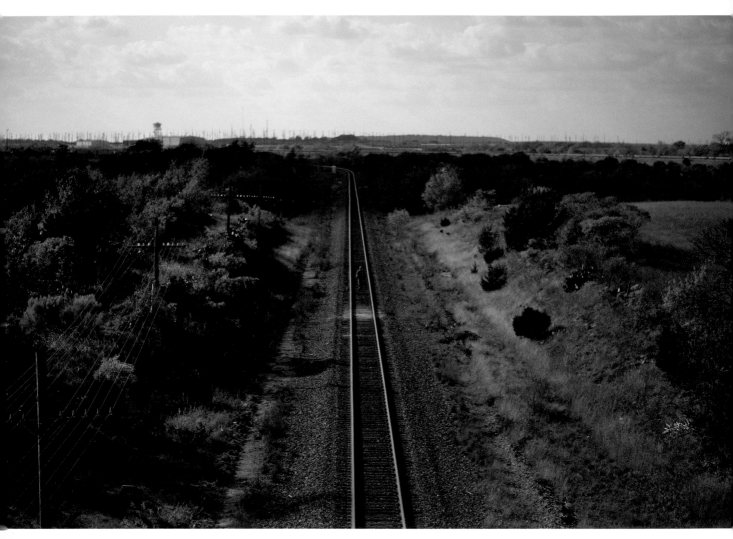

Ft. Hood, Texas 2009

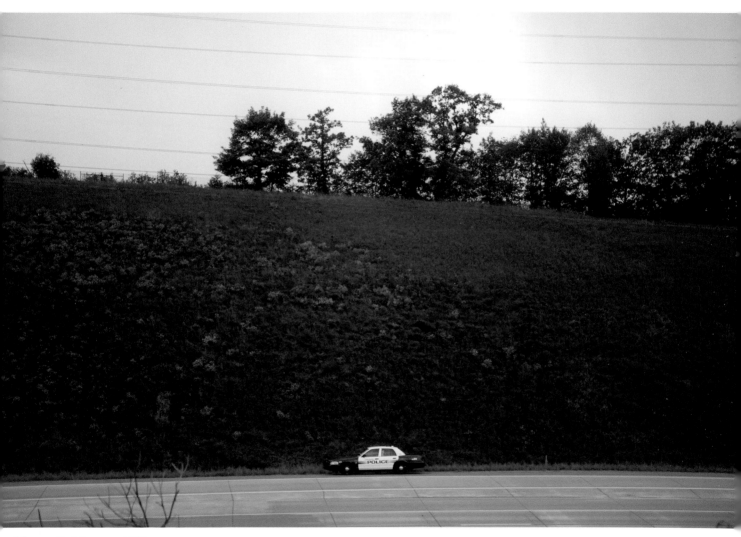

Minneapolis, Minnesota 2007

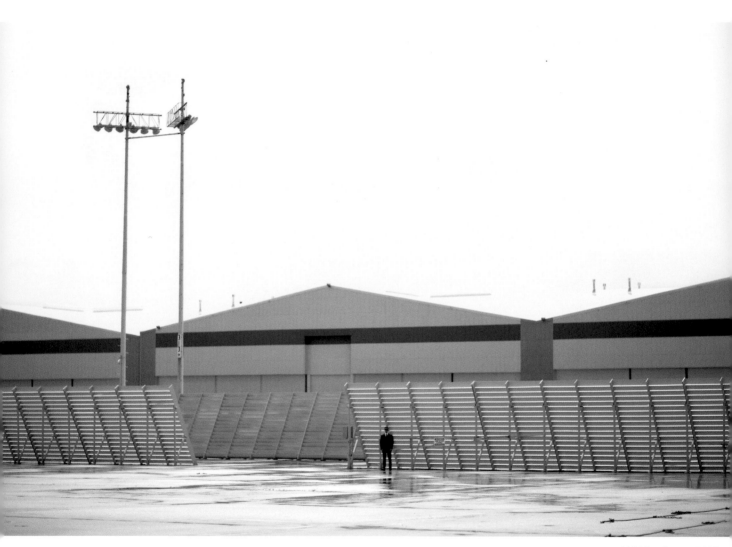

Wichita, Kansas 2007

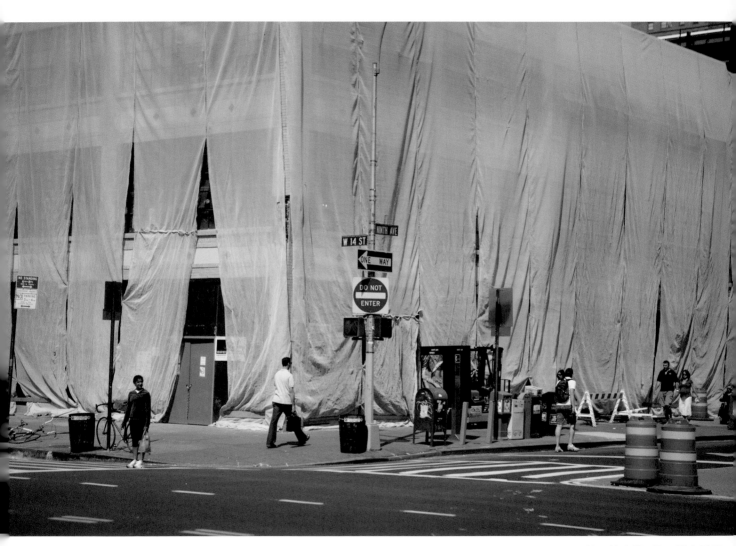

New York City, New York 2007

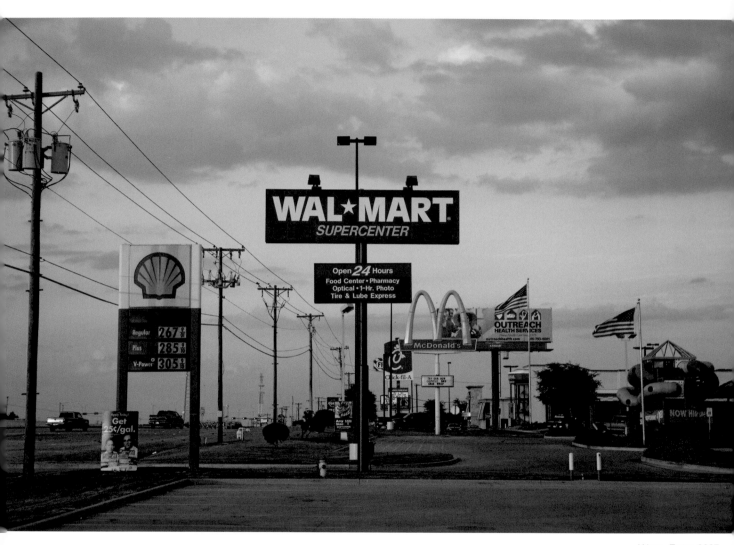

Waco, Texas 2007

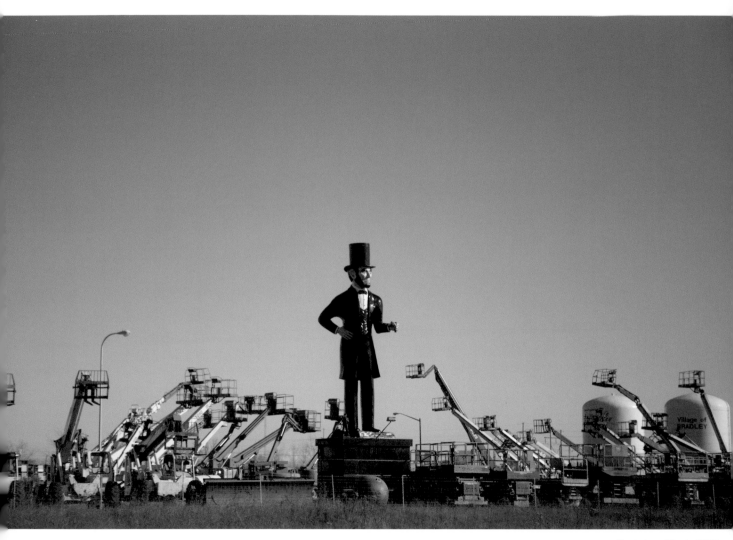

Kankakee, Illinois 2008

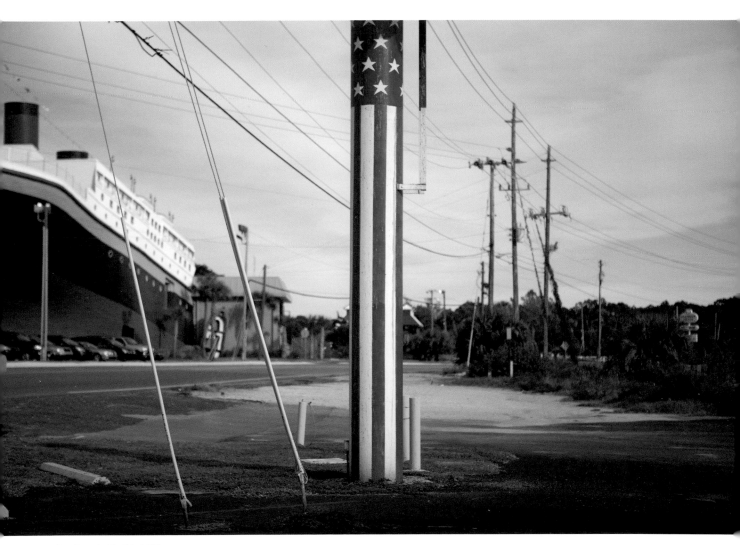

Panama City Beach, Florida 2009

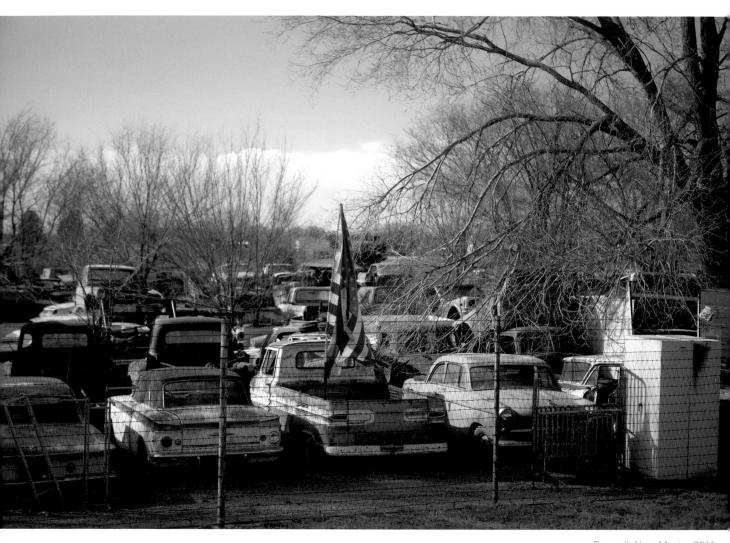

Roswell, New Mexico 2011

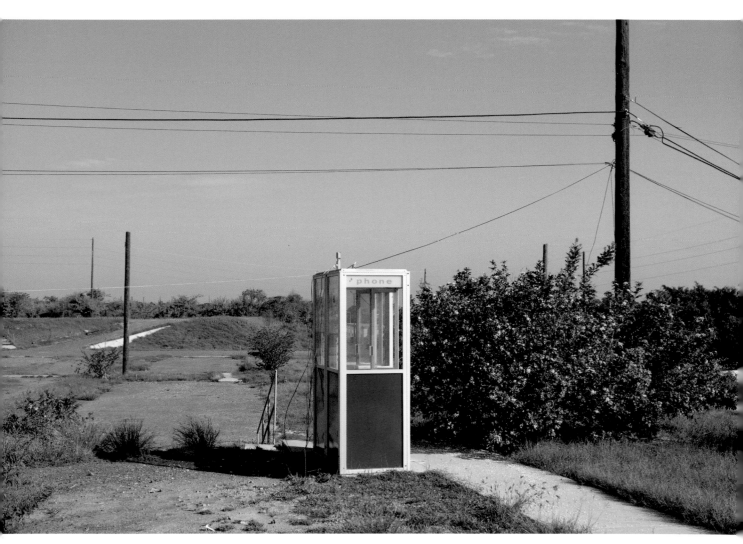

Guantanamo Bay, Cuba 2006

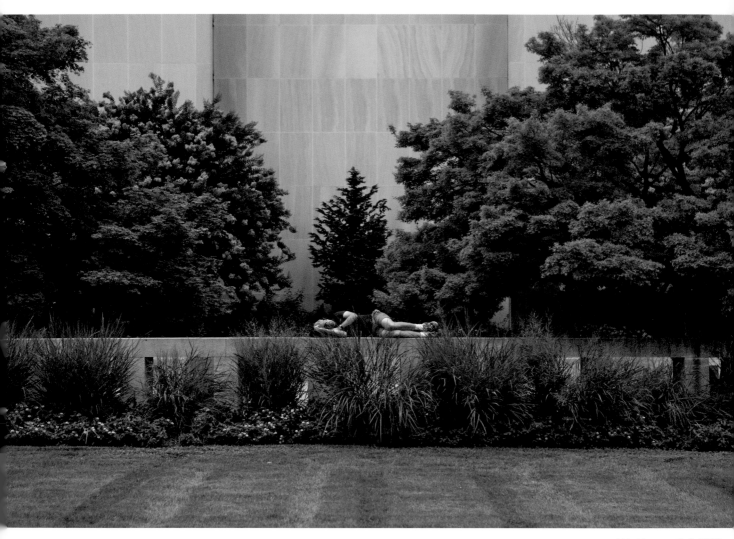

Washington, D.C. 2006

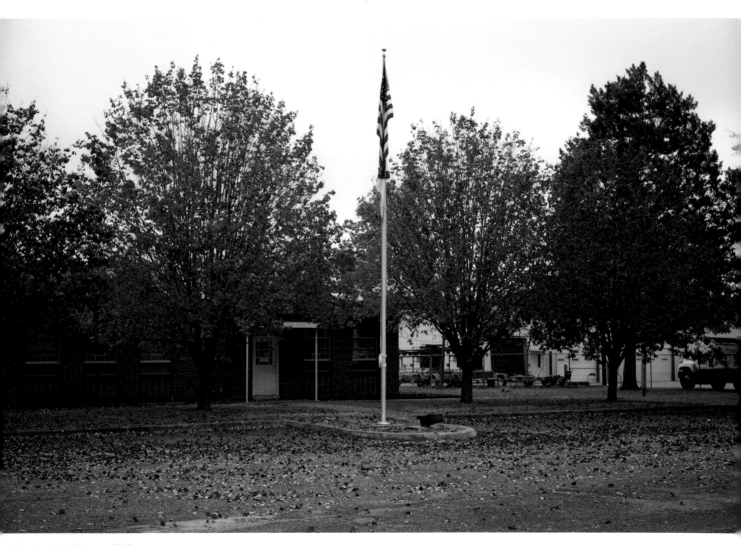

Maplesville, Alabama 2008

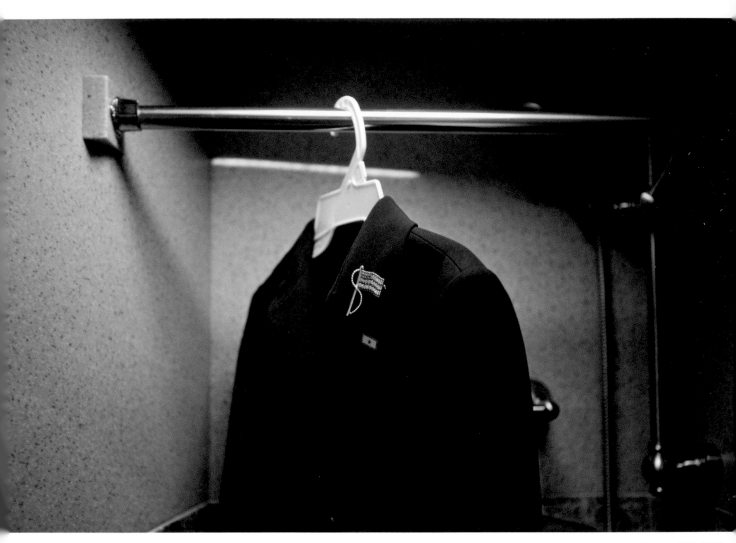

Dayton, Ohio 2008

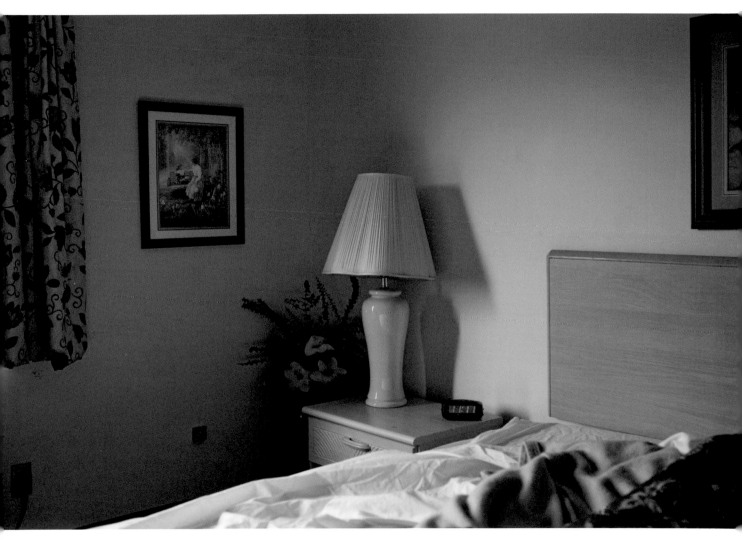

Steele, Missouri 2008

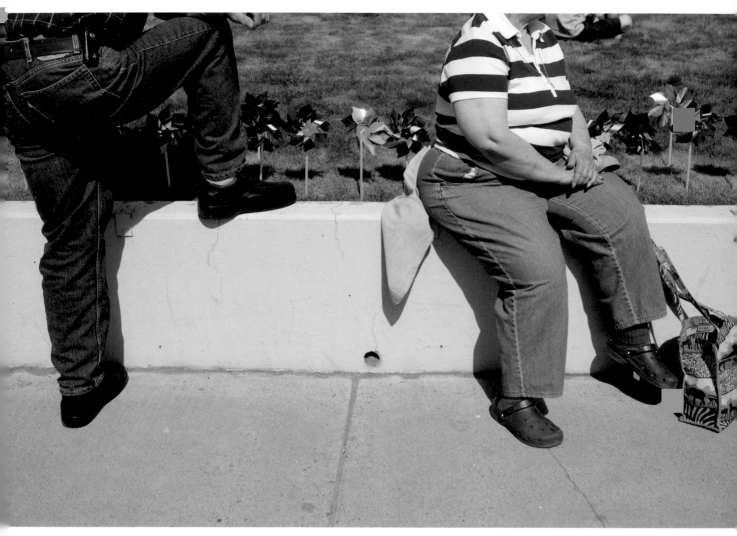

Elko, Nevada 2007

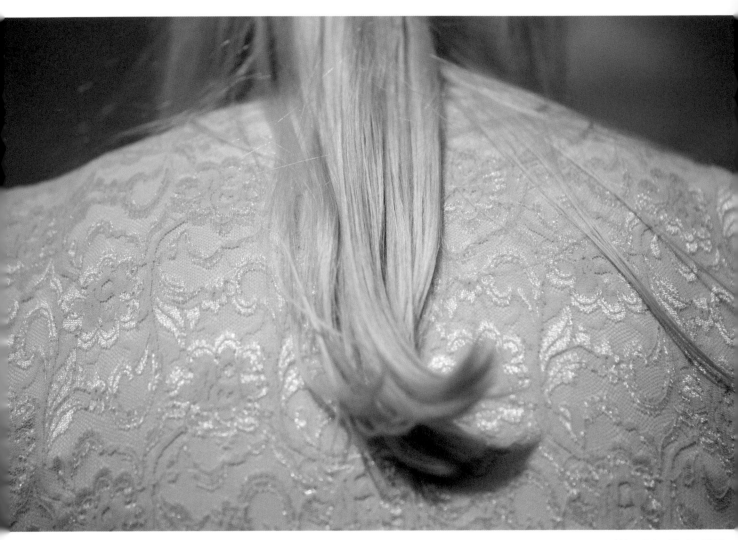

West Palm, Florida 2004

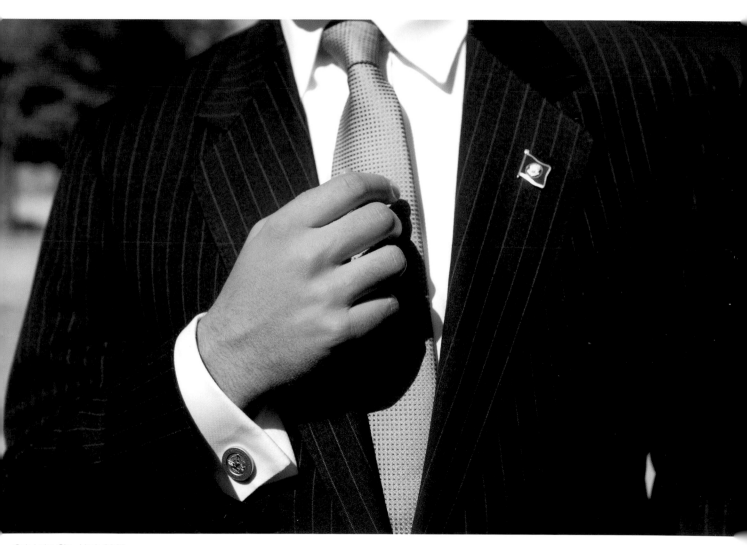

Salt Lake City, Utah 2006

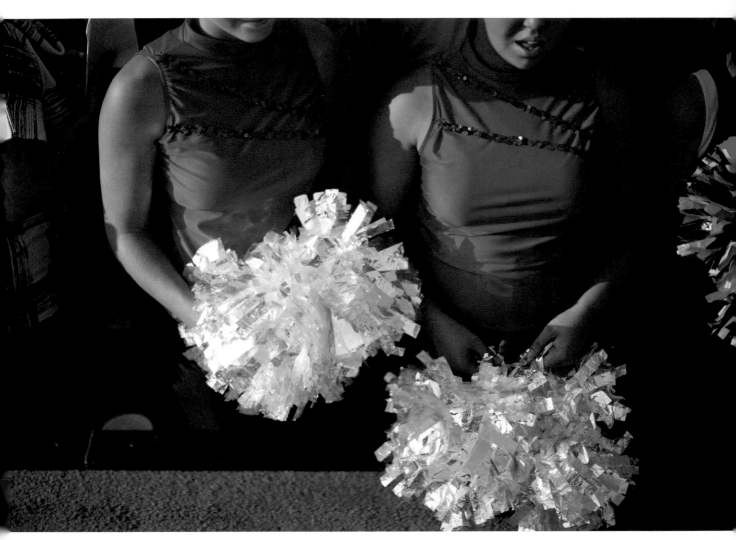

O'Fallon, Missouri 2008

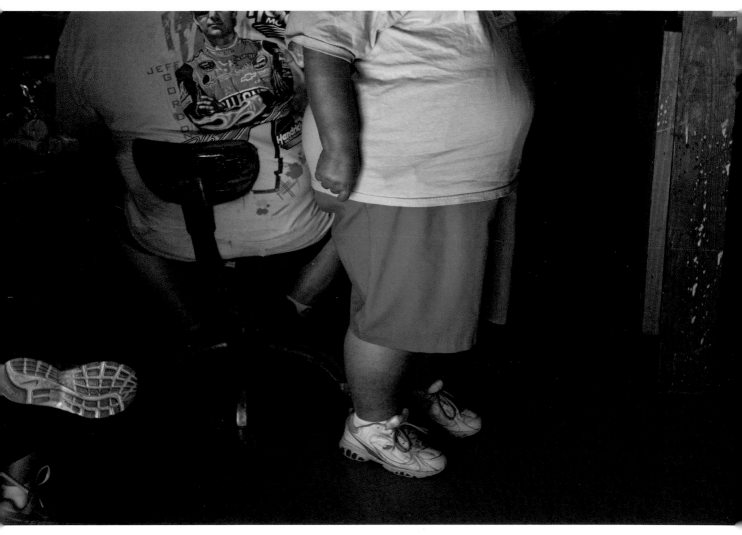

Obetz, Ohio 2008

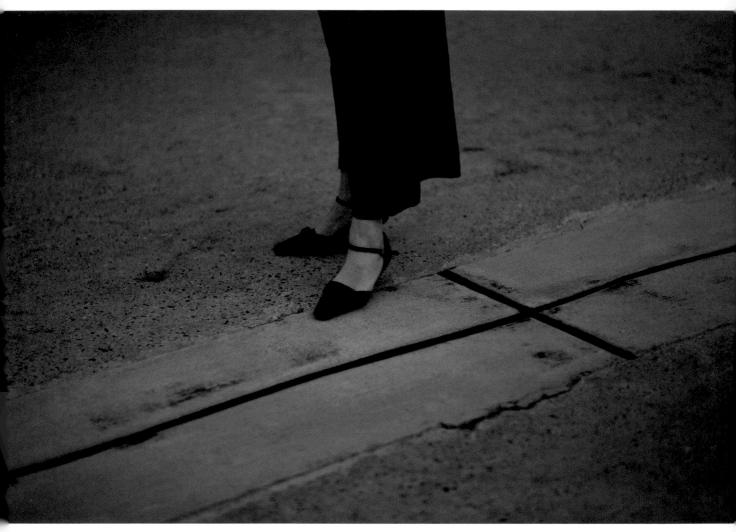

Andrews Air Force Base, Virginia 2007

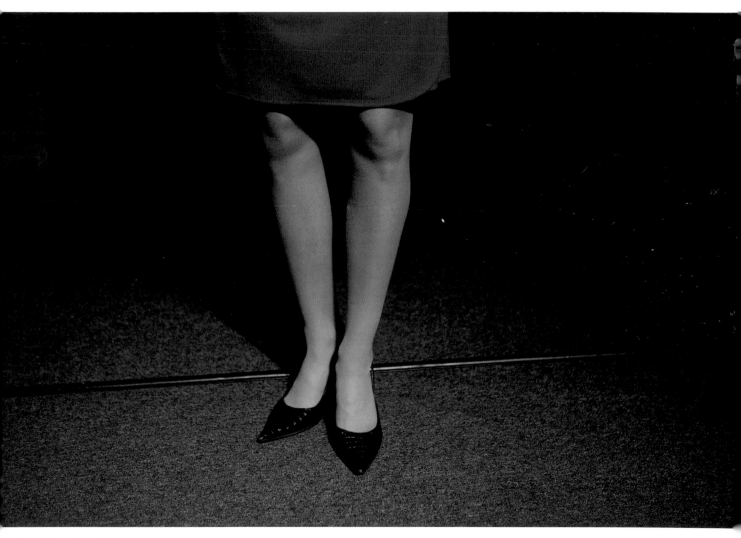

Des Moines, Iowa 2007

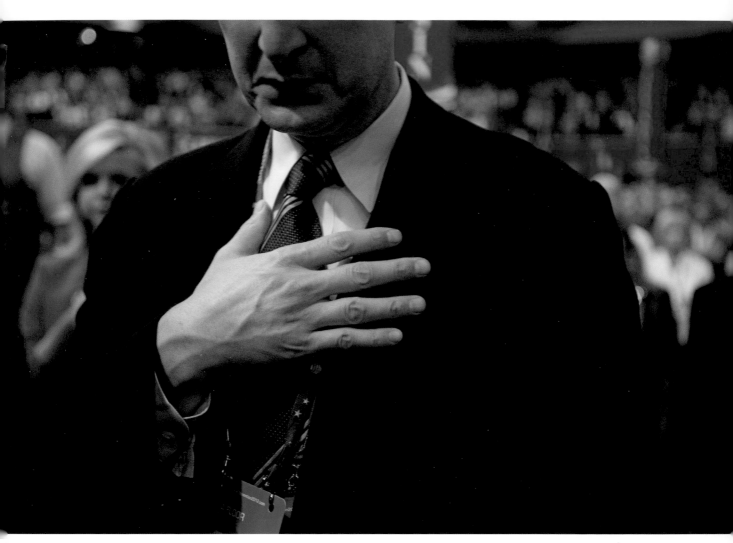

Tampa, Florida 2012

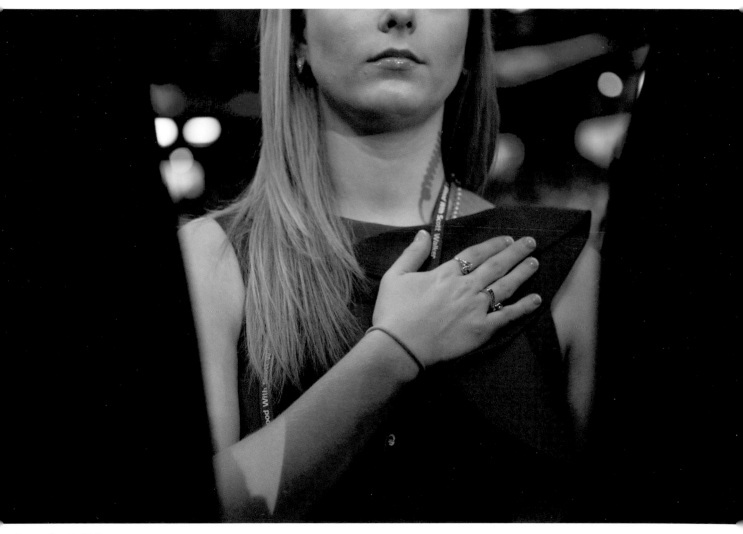

Tampa, Florida 2012

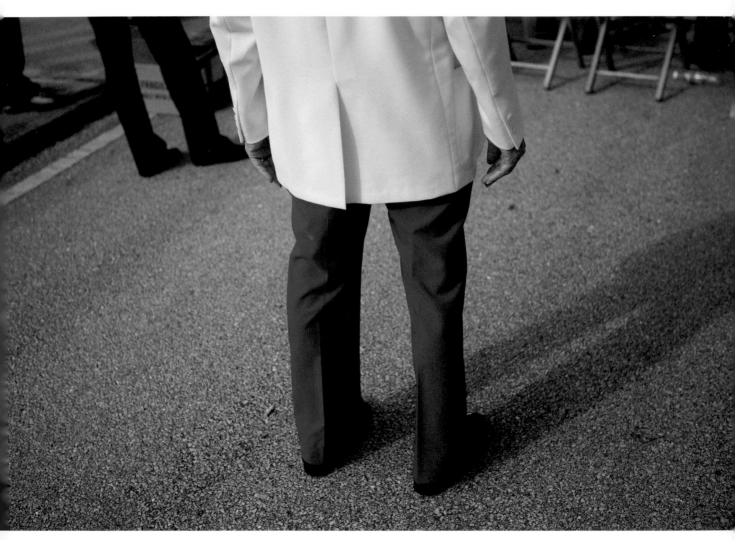

West Palm, Florida 2004

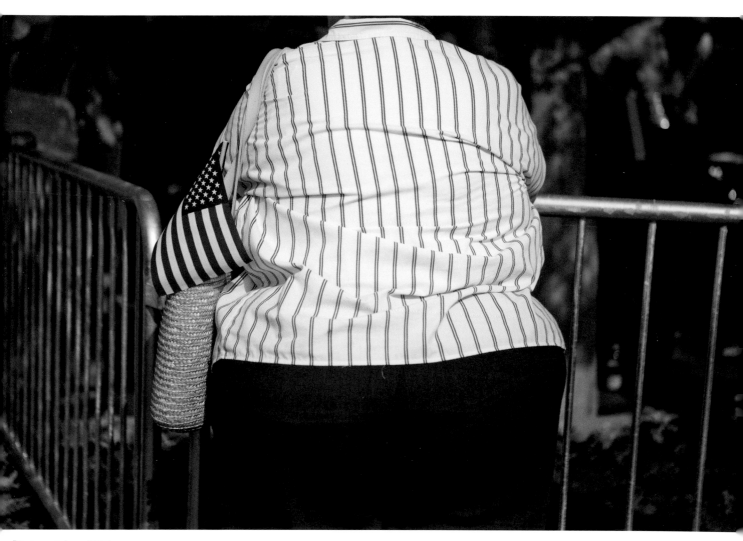

Davenport, Iowa 2007

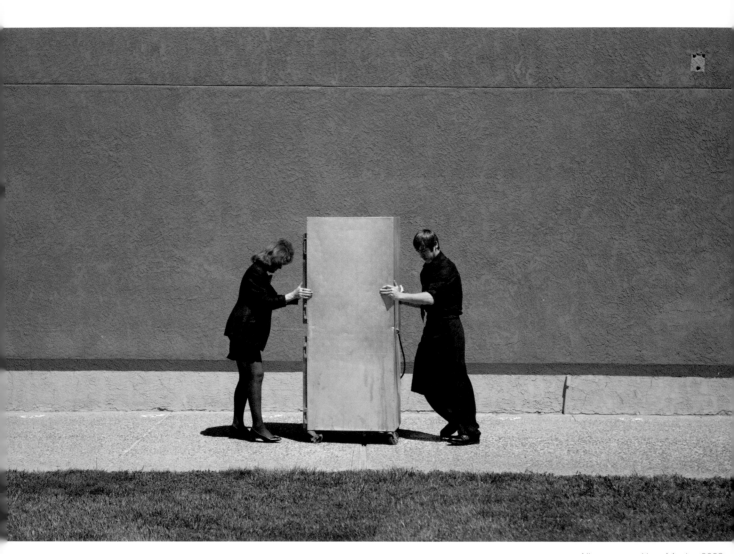

Albuquerque, New Mexico 2008

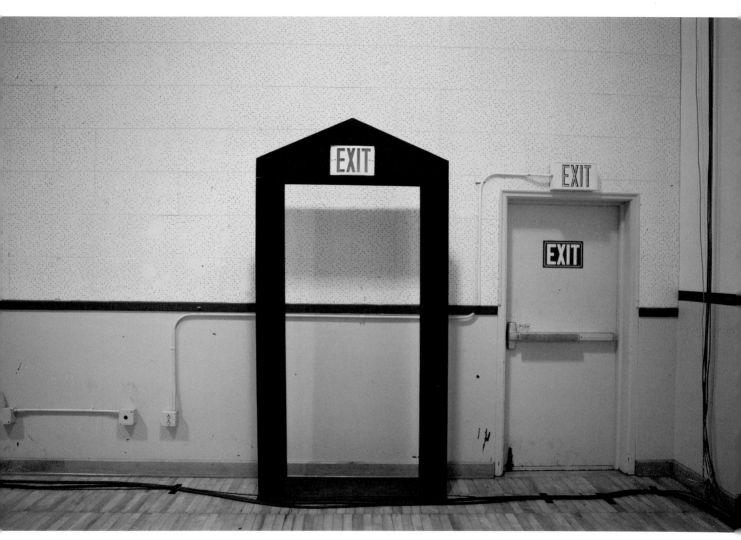

Burbank, California 2007

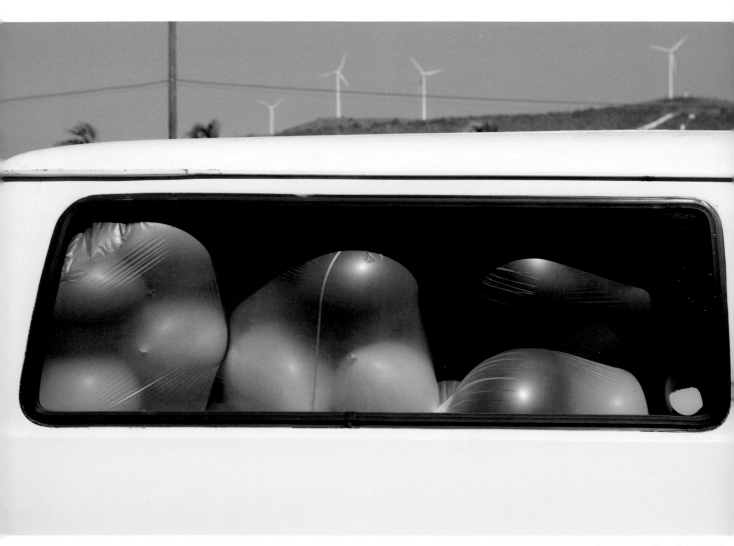

Guantanamo Bay, Cuba 2006

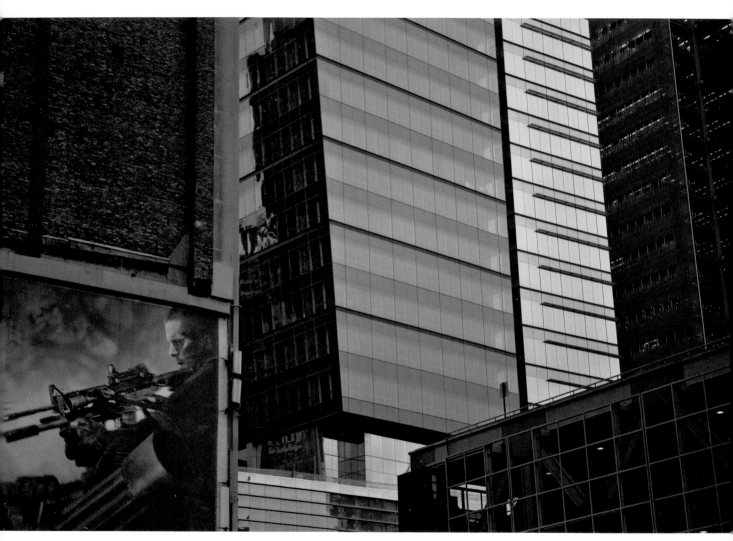

New York City, New York 2009

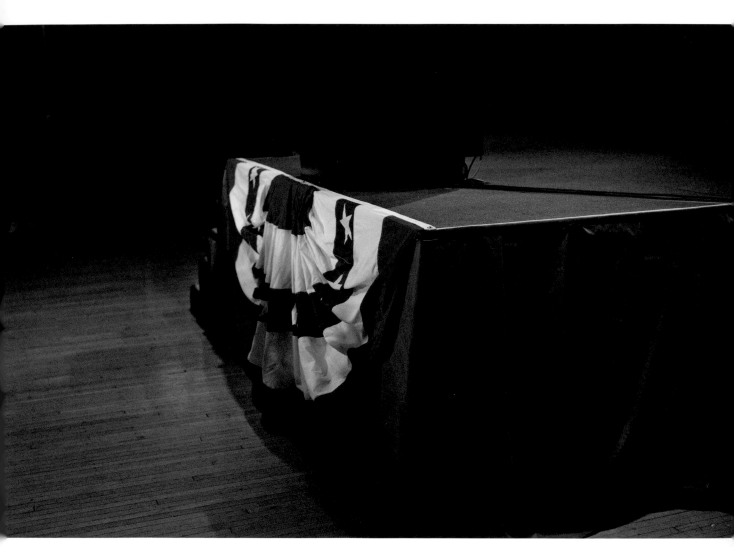

Des Moines, Iowa 2008

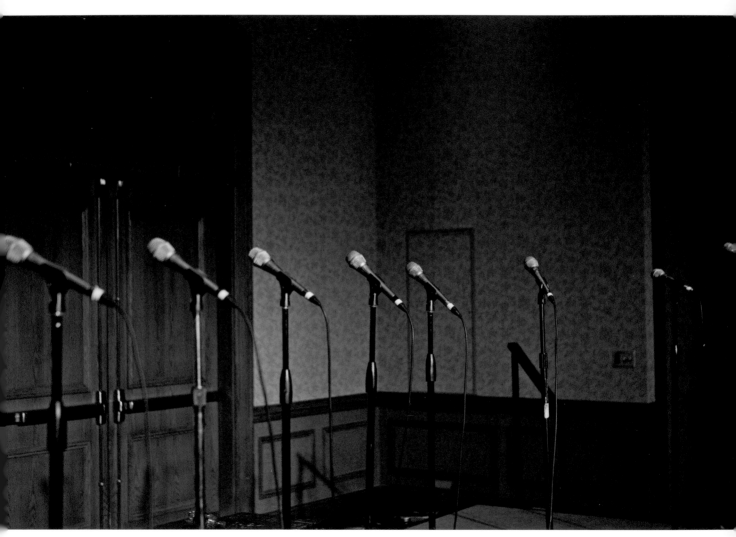

Minneapolis, Minnesota 2005

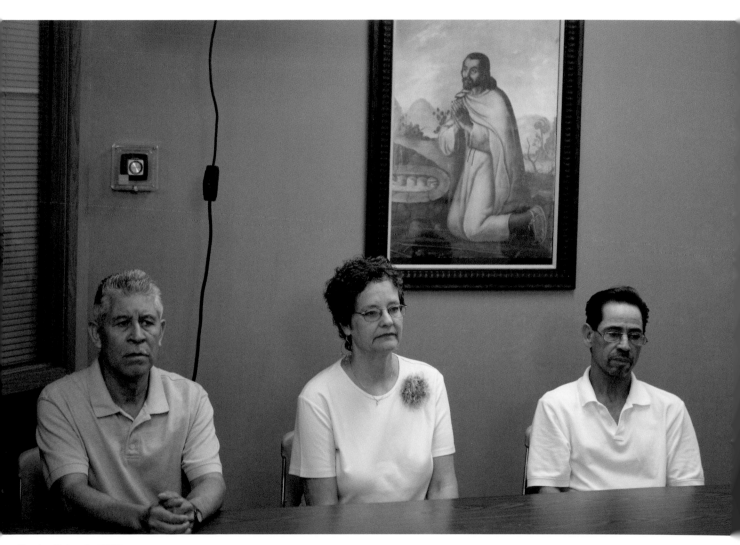

Omaha, Nebraska 2006

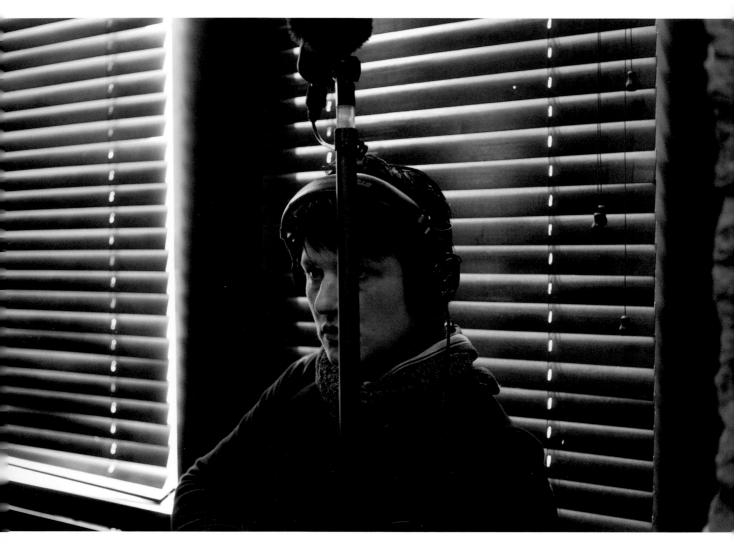

Ames, Iowa 2008

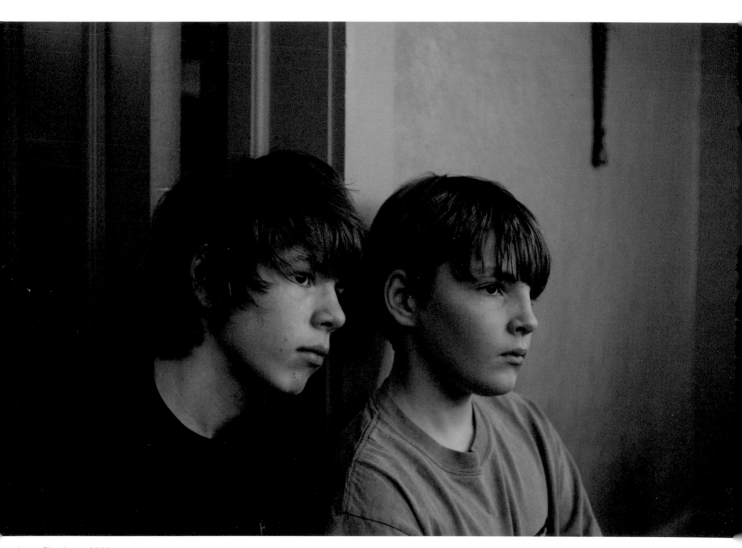

Iowa City, Iowa 2008

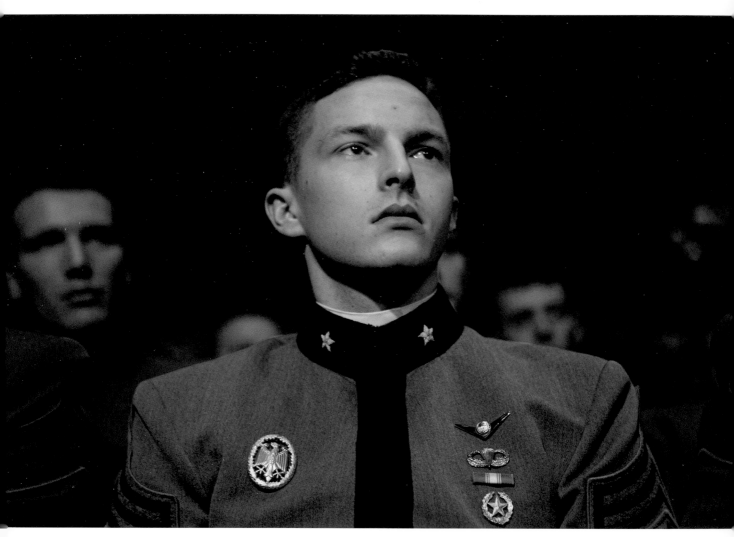

West Point, New York 2009

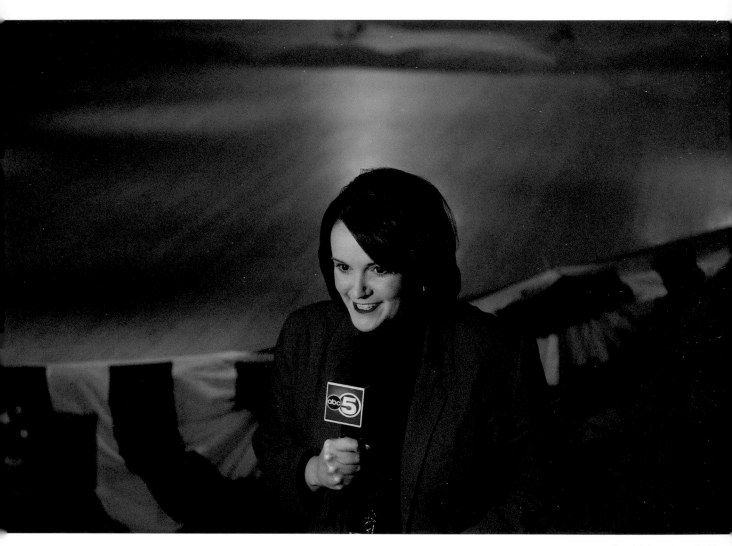

Des Moines, Iowa 2008

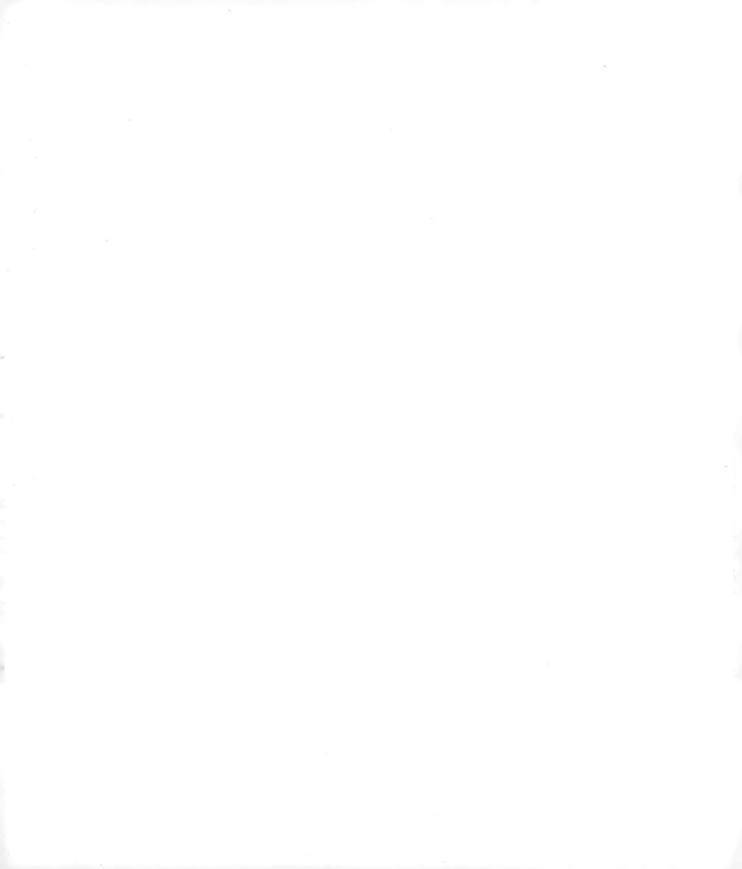

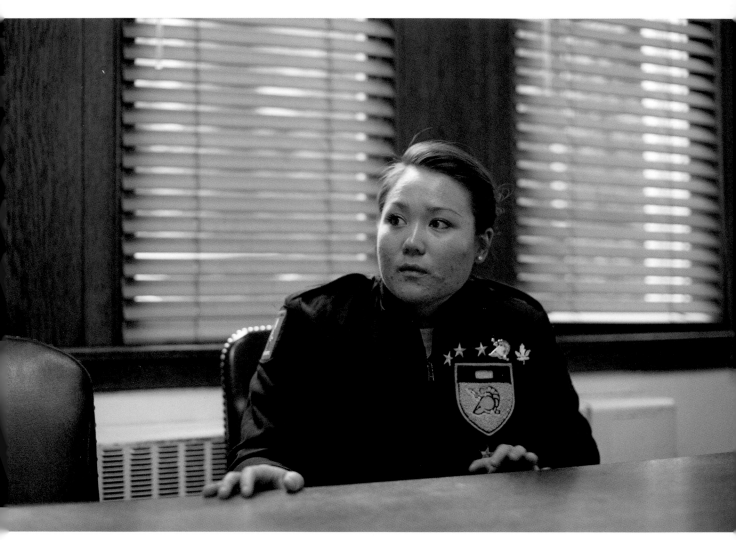

West Point, New York 2010

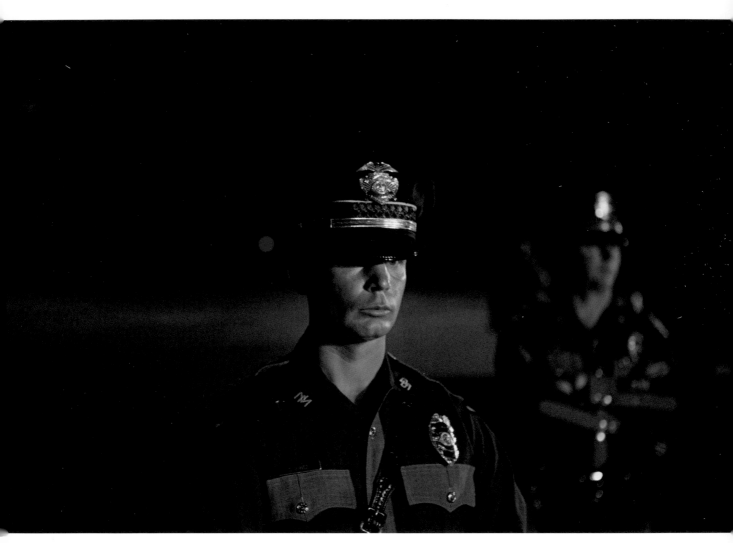

Roswell, New Mexico 2008

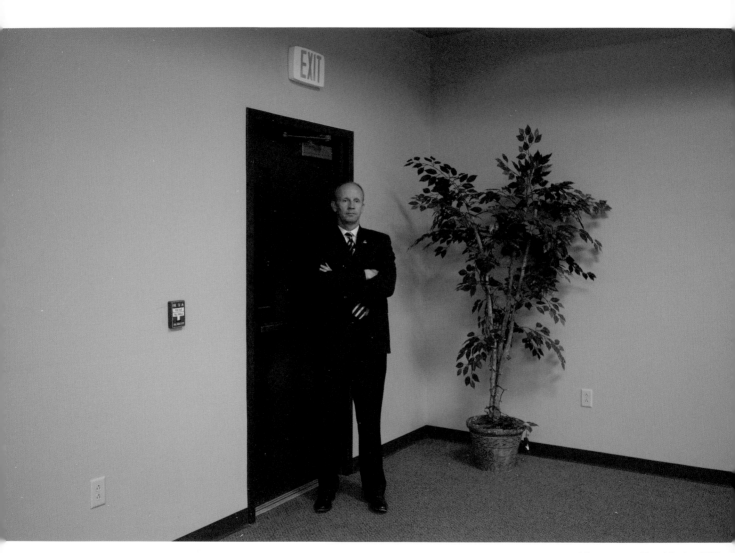

Albuquerque, New Mexico 2008

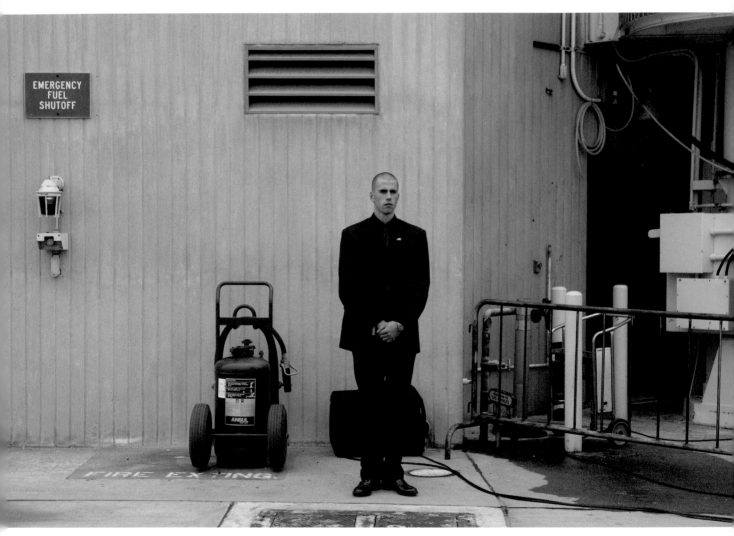

EMERGENCY
FUEL
SHUTOFF

Los Angeles, California 2005

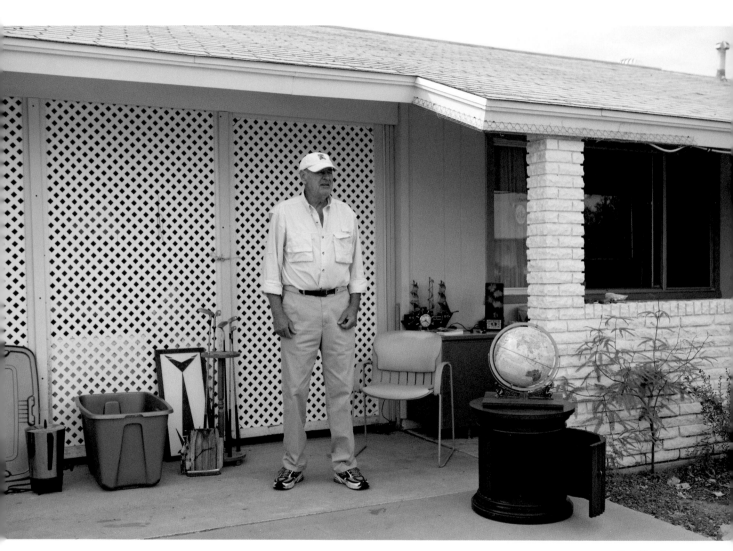

Sun City, Arizona 2010

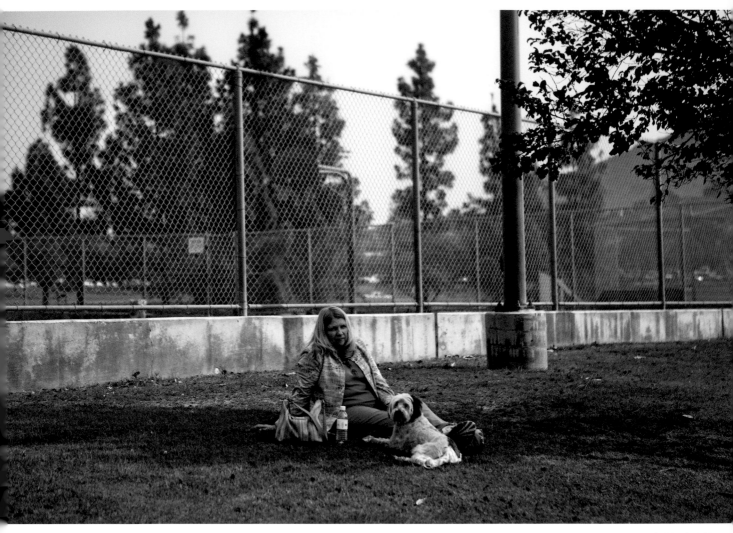

Escondia, California 2007

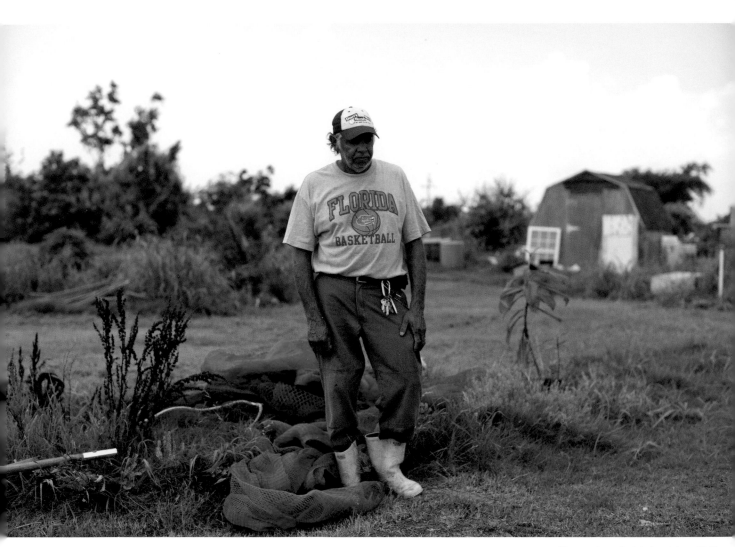

Plaquemines Parish, Louisiana 2010

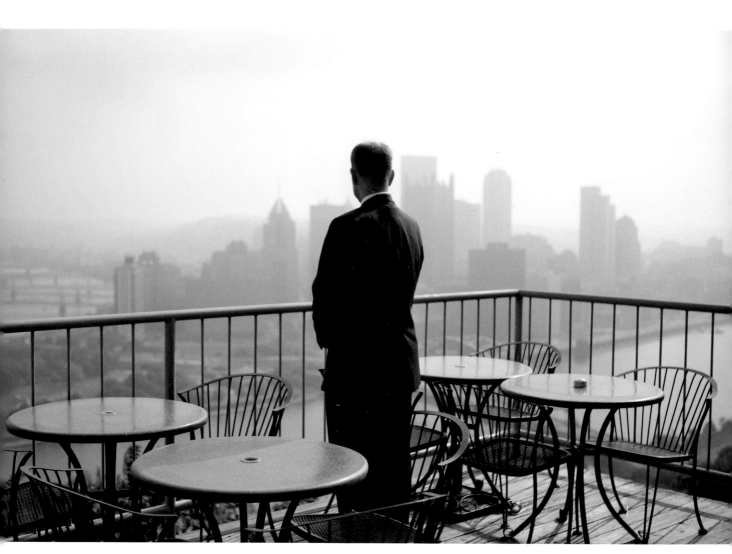

Washington, Pennsylvania 2008

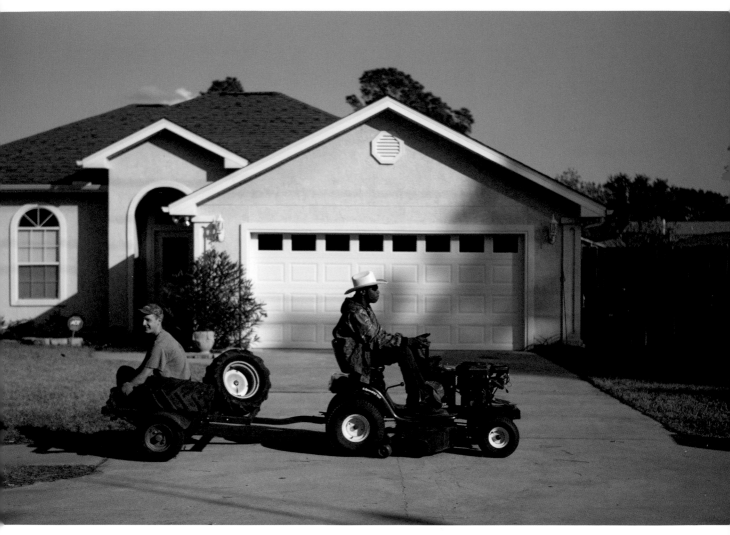

Callaway, Florida 2008

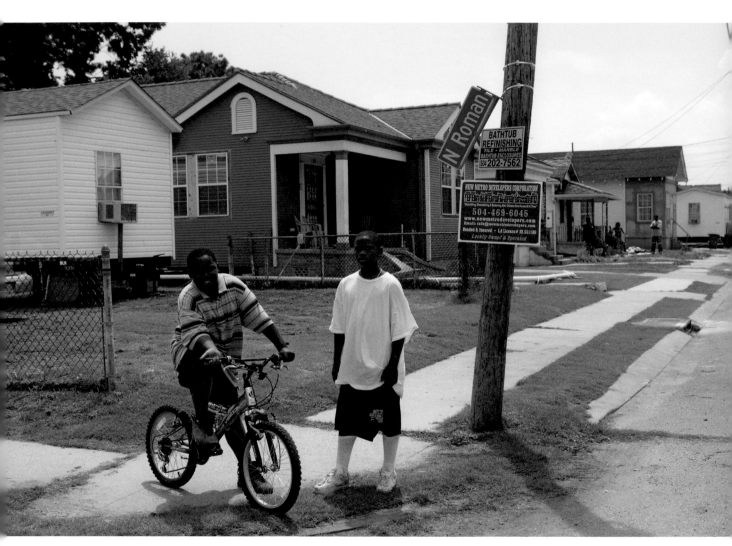

New Orleans, Louisiana 2006

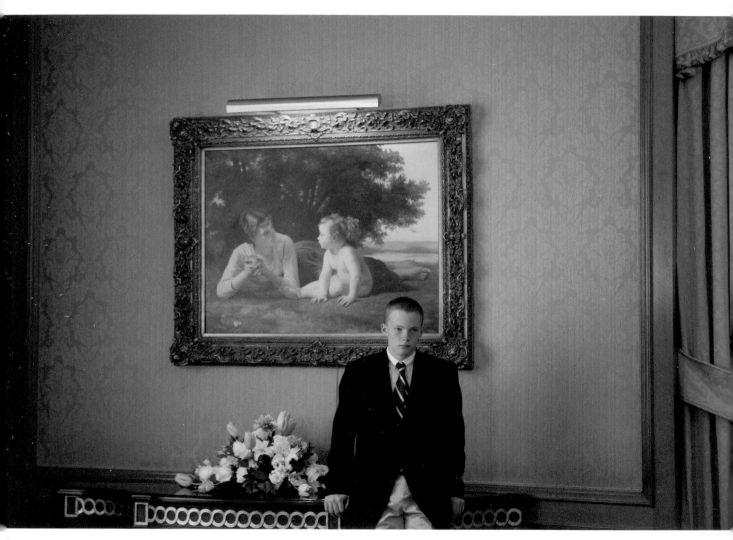

Salt Lake City, Utah 2008

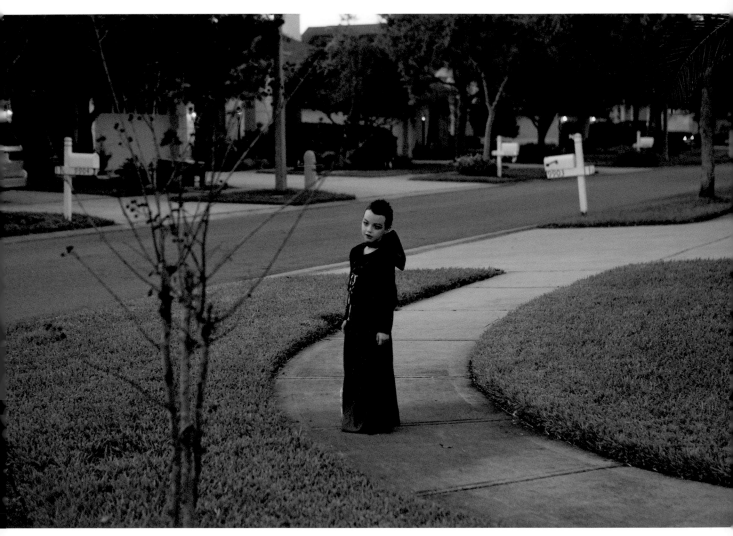

Tampa, Florida 2006

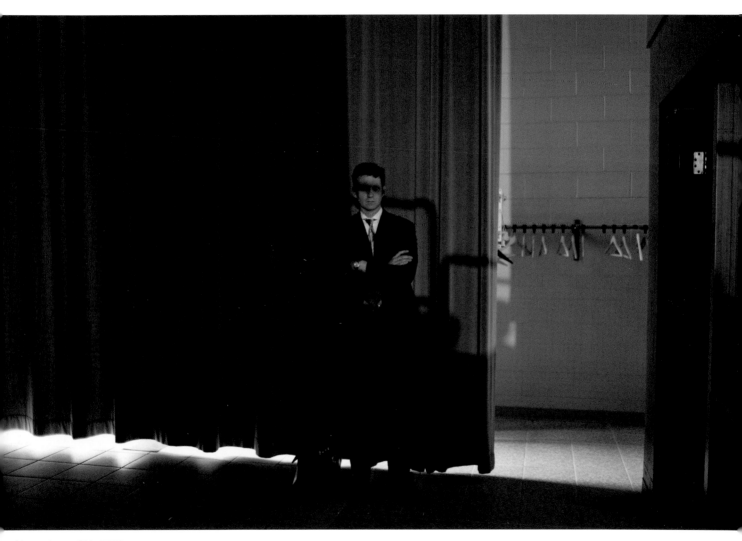

Youngstown, Ohio 2008

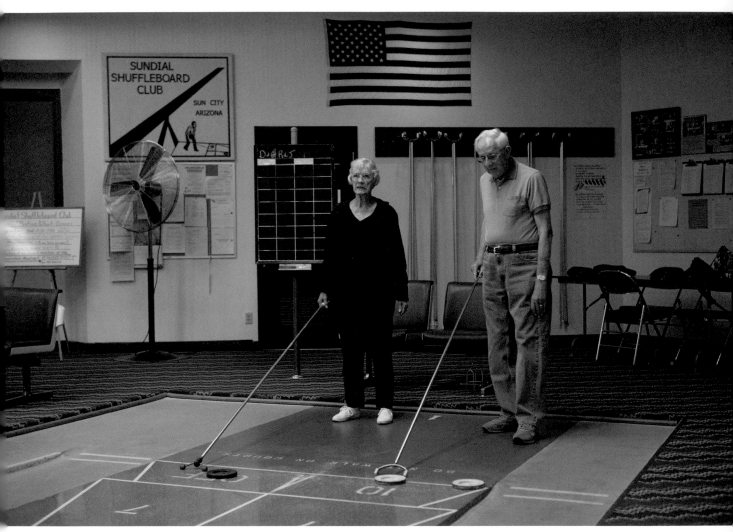

Sun City, Arizona 2010

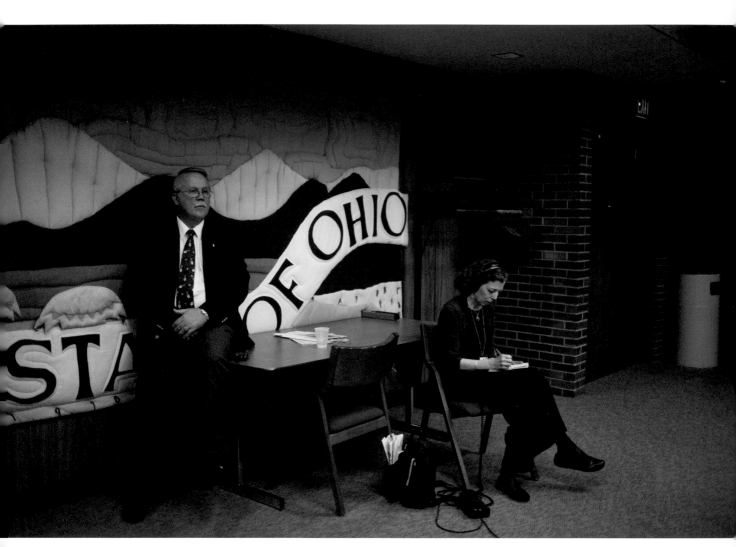

Youngstown, Ohio 2008

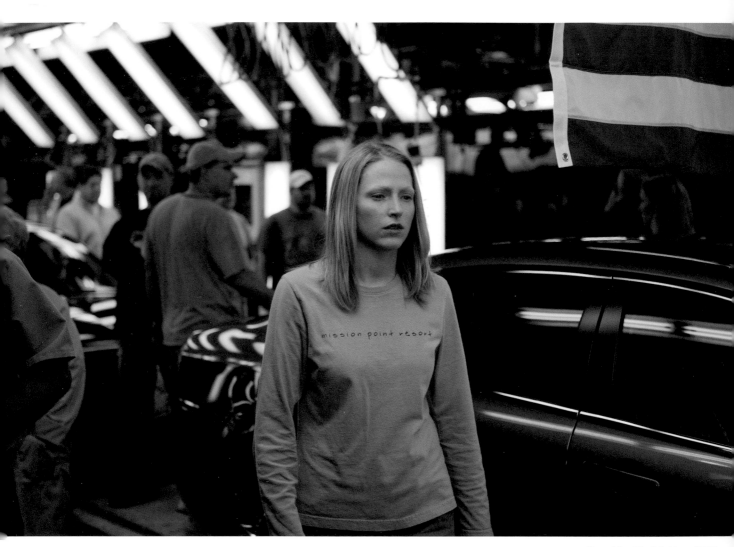

Grand Rapids, Michigan 2008

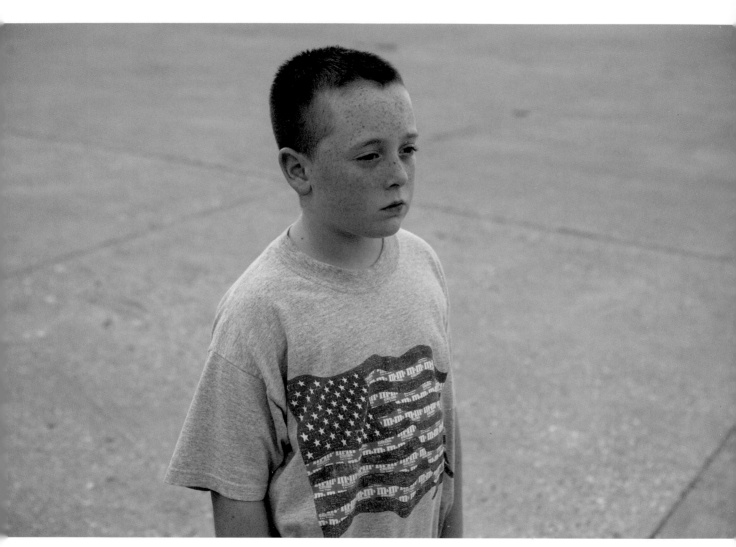

Guantanamo Bay, Cuba 2006

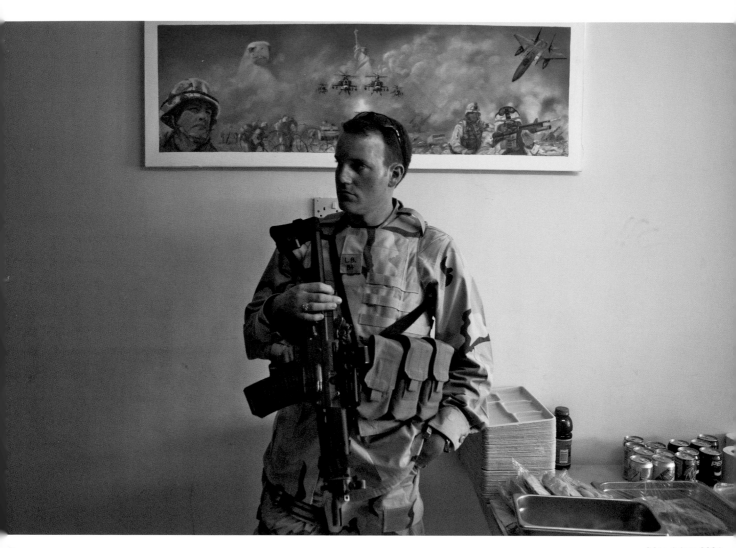

Mosul, Iraq 2004

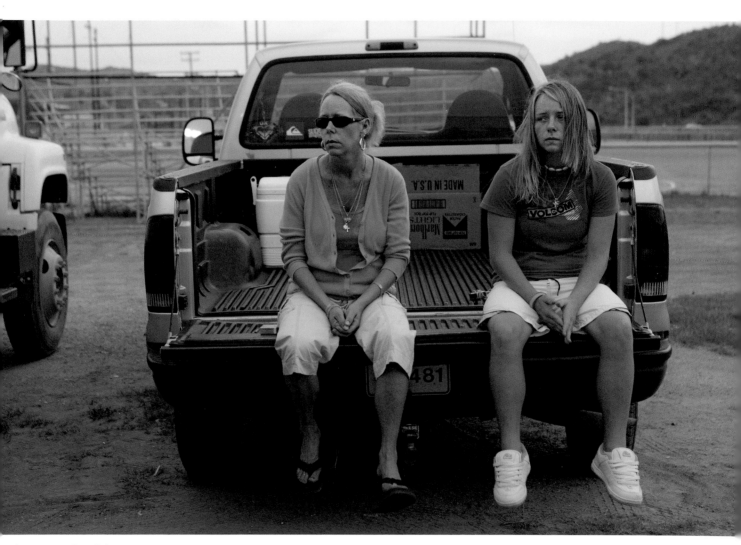

Guantanamo Bay, Cuba 2006

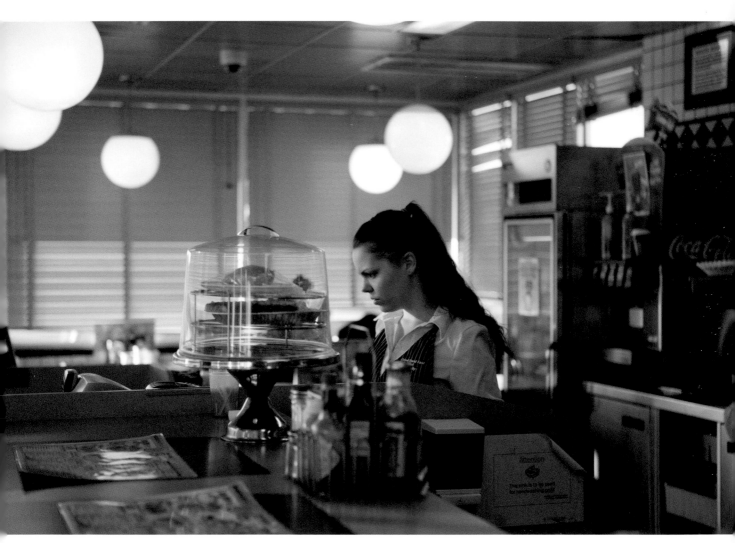

Battesville, Mississippi 2008

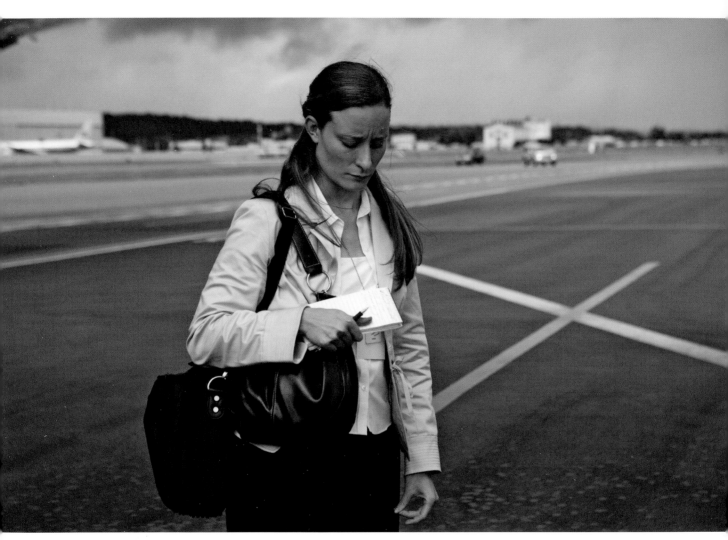

Seattle, Washington 2006

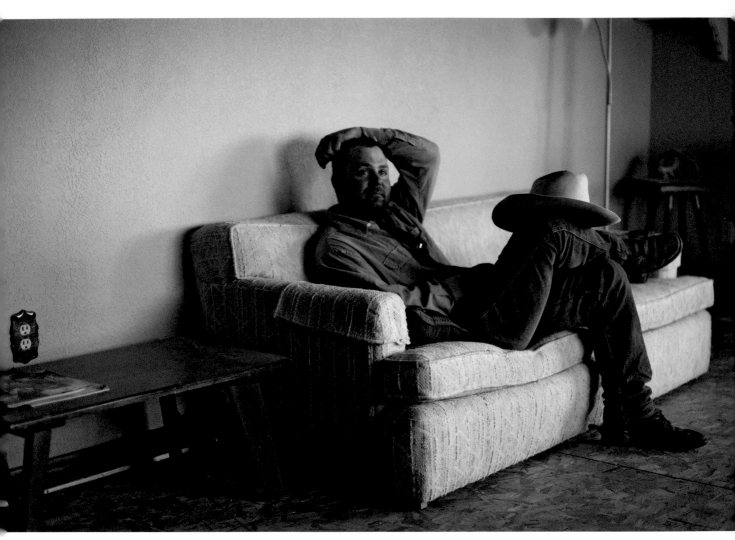

Apache, Arizona 2010

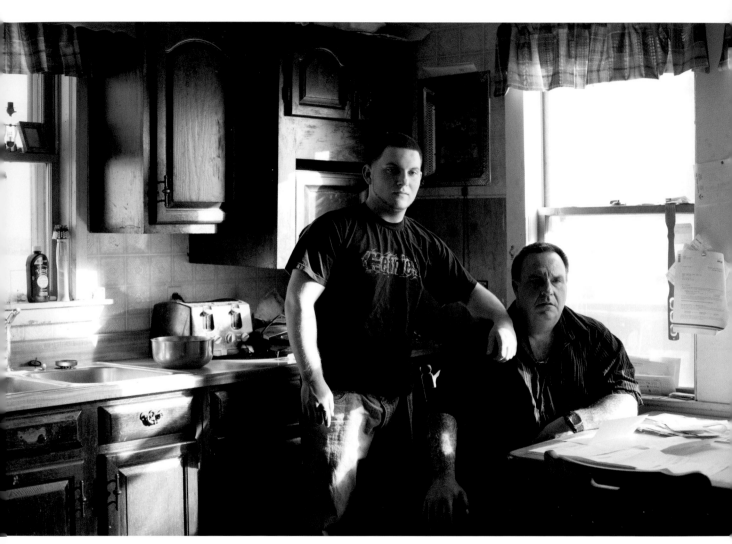

Methuen, Massachusetts 2010

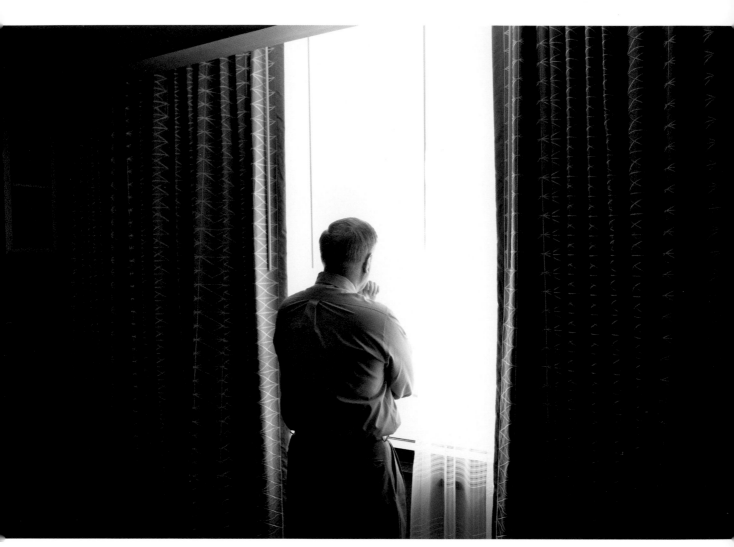

Minneapolis, Minnesota 2008

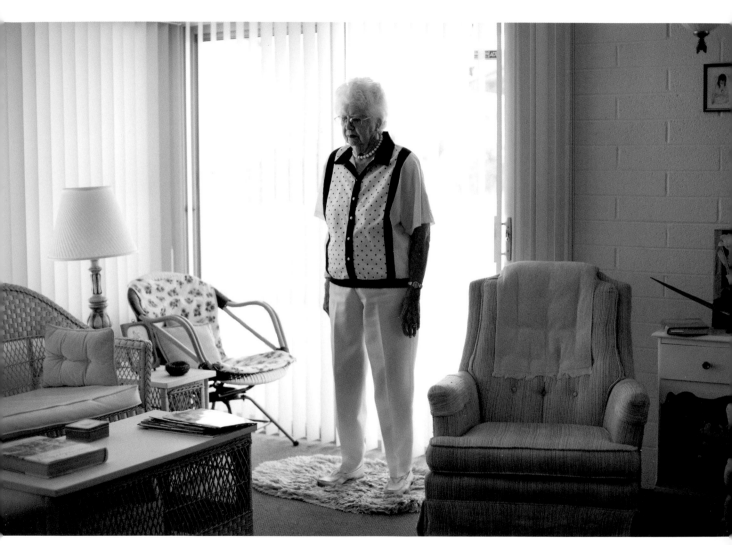

Sun City, Arizona 2010

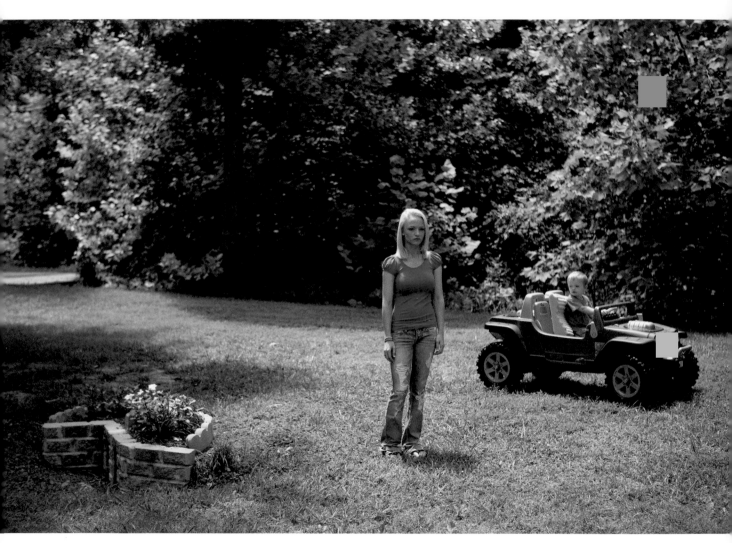

Ooltewah, Tennessee 2011

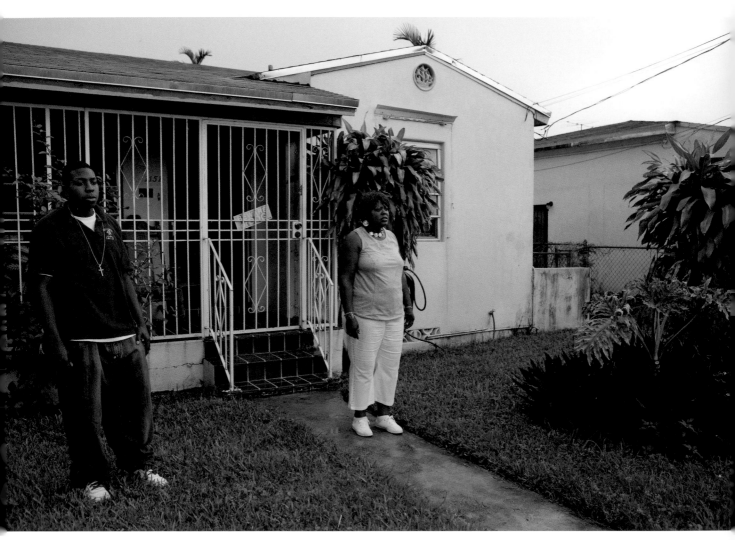

Liberty City, Florida 2006

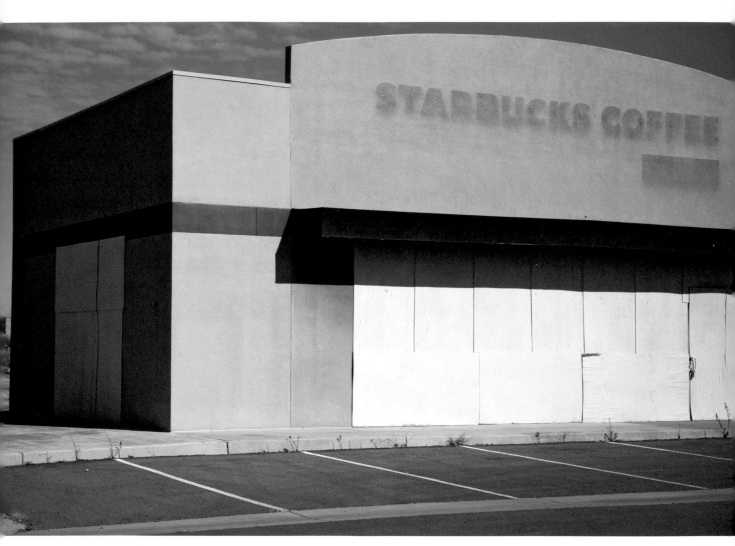

Roswell, New Mexico 2011

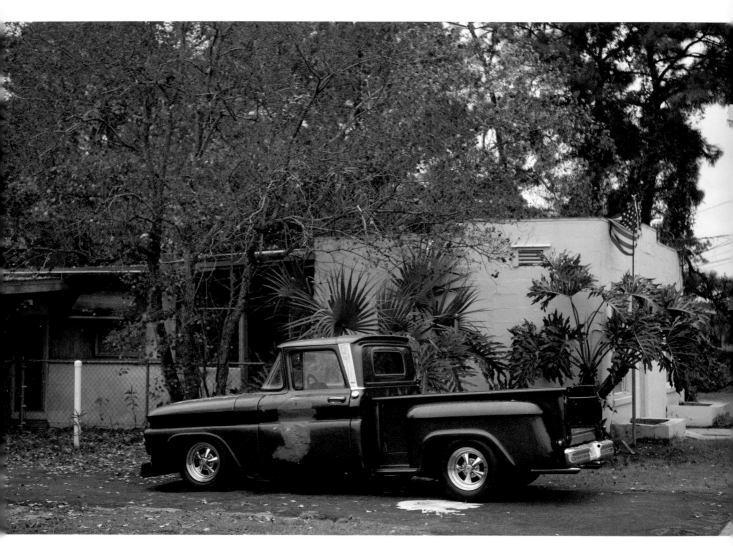

Panama City Beach, Florida 2008

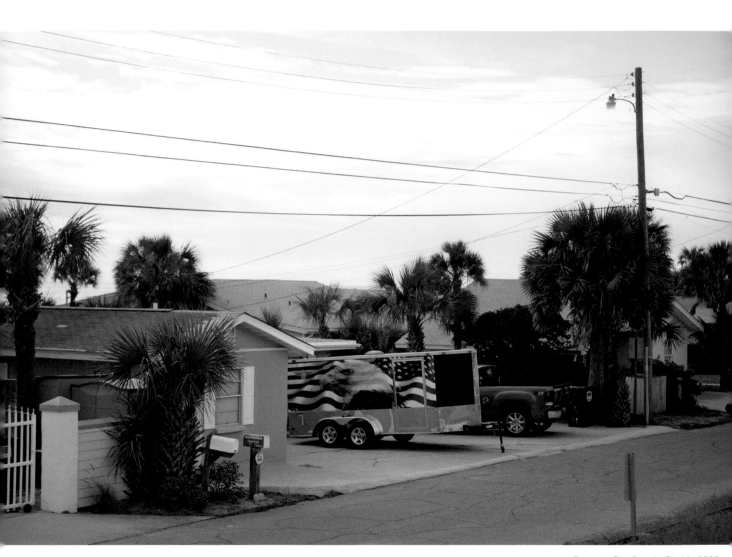

Panama City Beach, Florida 2009

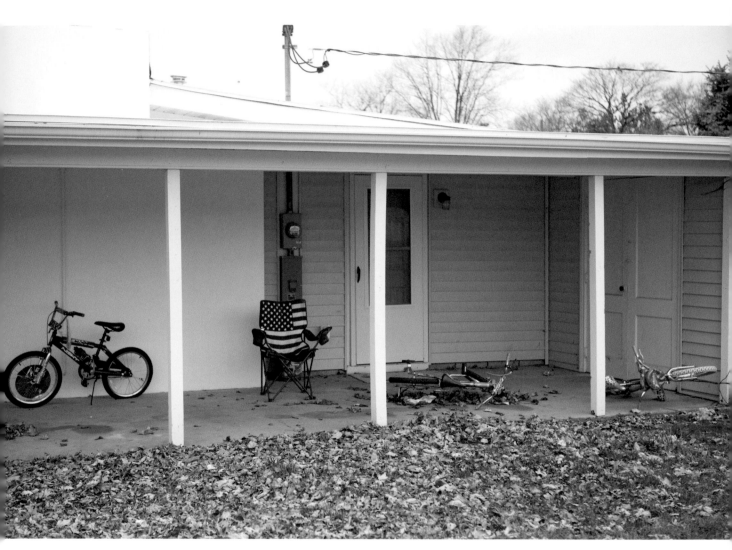

Arcola, Illinois 2008

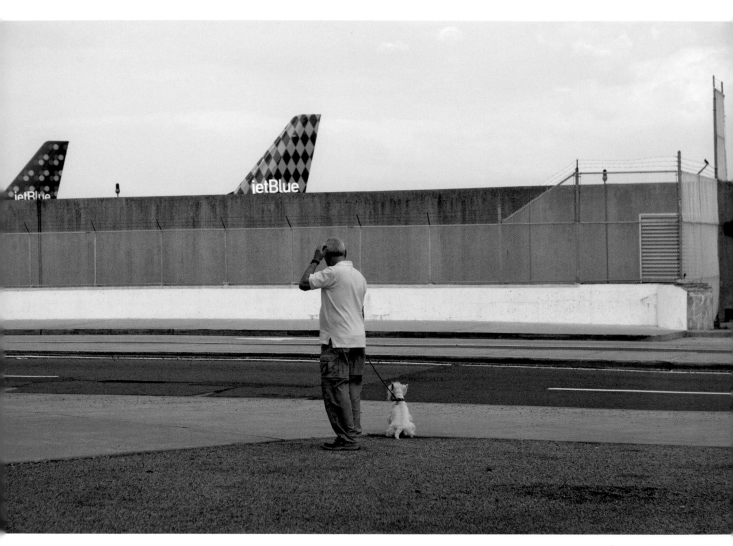

Queens, New York 2006

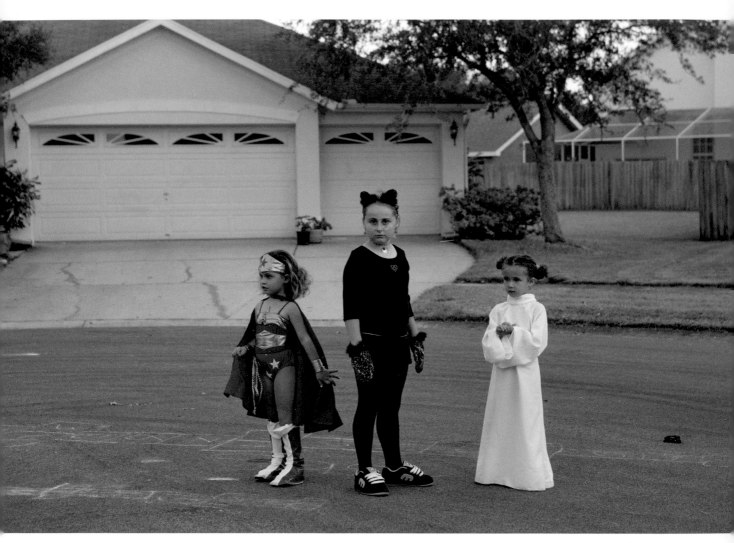

Tampa, Florida 2005

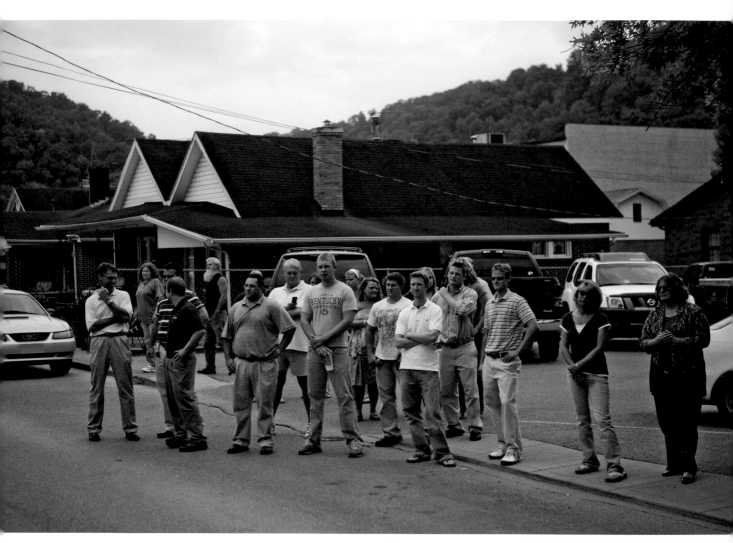

Prestonsburg, Kentucky 2007

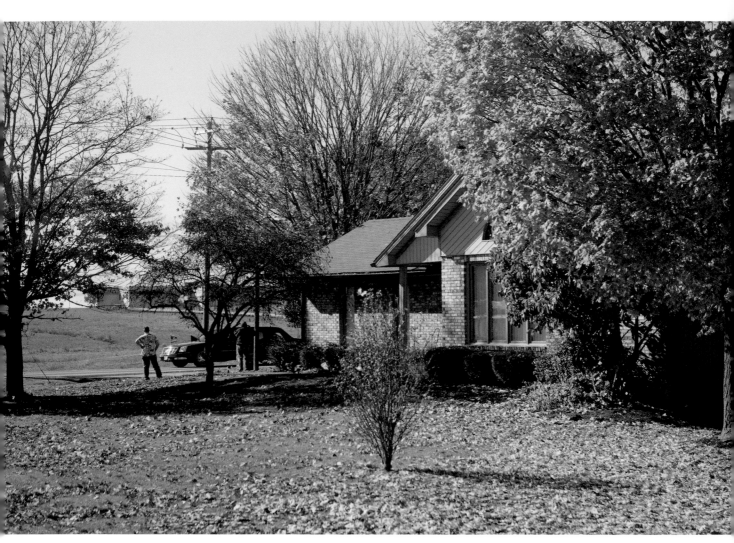

Sellersburg, Indiana 2006

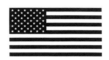

ANNUIT COEPTIS

"HE HAS FAVORED OUR UNDERTAKINGS"

depression

noun

1 *she seems to be suffering from depression*: unhappiness, sadness, melancholy, melancholia, misery, sorrow, woe, gloom, despondency, low spirits, a heavy heart, despair, desolation, hopelessness; upset, tearfulness; informal the dumps, the doldrums, the blues, a funk, a blue funk; Psychiatry dysthymia, seasonal affective disorder, SAD.

2 *an economic depression*: recession, slump, decline, downturn, standstill; stagnation; the Great Depression; Economics stagflation.

AMERICANS

CHRISTOPHER MORRIS

STEIDL

Dedicated to my Father Curtis
Mr. Mo
(1935-2011)

AMERICANS